DEMCO

Primary Source Accounts of the

Korean War

JOHN RICHARD CONWAY, ESQ.

MyReportLinks.com Books

an imprint of

Enslow Publishers, Inc. E

Box 398, 40 Industrial Road
Berkeley Heights, NJ 07922
USA

*The author and editors gratefully acknowledge
Catherine Neville, Major, U.S. Army Nurse Corps,
and Martin Lorenz, Sergeant, U.S. Army 7th Infantry Division,
veterans of the Korean War, for their contributions to this book
and for their service to their country.*

MyReportLinks.com Books, an imprint of Enslow Publishers, Inc. MyReportLinks®
is a registered trademark of Enslow Publishers, Inc.

Library of Congress Cataloging-in-Publication Data

Conway, John Richard, 1969–
  Primary source accounts of the Korean War / John Richard Conway.
    p. cm. — (America's wars through primary sources)
  Includes bibliographical references and index.
  ISBN 1-59845-003-4
  1. Korean War, 1950–1953—Juvenile literature. 2. Korean War, 1950–1953—United States—
Juvenile literature. I. Title. II. Series.
  DS918.C68 2006
  951.904'28—dc22
                            2006000216

Printed in the United States of America

10 9 8 7 6 5 4 3 2 1

To Our Readers:
Through the purchase of this book, you and your library gain access to the Report Links that specifically
back up this book. The Publisher will provide access to the Report Links that back up this book and will
keep these Report Links up to date on **www.myreportlinks.com** for five years from the book's first
publication date.
We have done our best to make sure all Internet addresses in this book were active and appropriate when
we went to press. However, the author and the Publisher have no control over, and assume no liability
for, the material available on those Internet sites or on other Web sites they may link to.
The usage of the MyReportLinks.com Books Web site is subject to the terms and conditions stated on the
Usage Policy Statement on **www.myreportlinks.com.**
A password may be required to access the Report Links that back up this book. The password is found
on the bottom of page 4 of this book.
Any comments or suggestions can be sent by e-mail to comments@myreportlinks.com or to the address
on the back cover.

Photo Credits: See page 128.

Cover Photo: A machine-gun crew with the U.S. Army's 2nd Infantry Division locates North Korean
forces near the Chongchon River, November 1950; National Archives and Records Administration/
Department of Defense.

Every effort has been made to locate all copyright holders of material used in this book. If any errors or
omissions have occurred, please contact us at www.myreportlinks.com. We will try to make corrections
in future editions.

CONTENTS

About MyReportLinks.com Books   4

What Are Primary Sources?   5

Time Line of the Korean War   6

Korea in 1953 Map   8

1   A Stand at Pork Chop Hill   9

2   A Brief History of the Korean War 20

3   Life on the Front 56

4   Under Fire and Imprisoned 70

5   The Politics of War
     and the American Public 86

6   Coming Home 98

7   Aftermath 107

     Report Links 116

     Glossary 118

     Chapter Notes 120

     Further Reading 125

     Index 126

MyReportLinks.com Books
Great Books, Great Links, Great for Research!

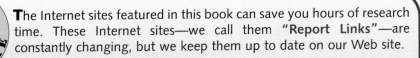

The Internet sites featured in this book can save you hours of research time. These Internet sites—we call them **"Report Links"**—are constantly changing, but we keep them up to date on our Web site.

When you see this "Approved Web Site" logo, you will know that we are directing you to a great Internet site that will help you with your research.

Give it a try! Type http://www.myreportlinks.com into your browser, click on the series title and enter the password, then click on the book title, and scroll down to the Report Links listed for this book.

The Report Links will bring you to great source documents, photographs, and illustrations. MyReportLinks.com Books save you time, feature Report Links that are kept up to date, and make report writing easier than ever! A complete listing of the Report Links can be found on pages 116–117 at the back of the book.

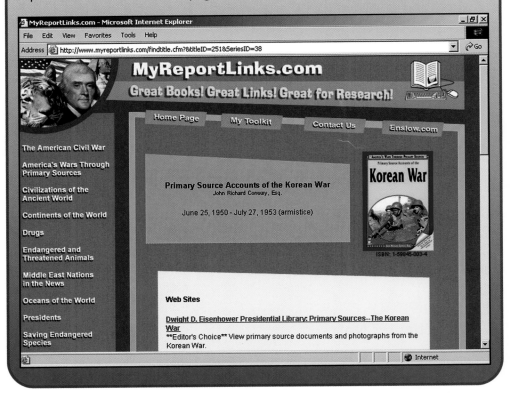

Please see "To Our Readers" on the copyright page for important information about this book, the MyReportLinks.com Web site, and the Report Links that back up this book.

Please enter PKW1807 if asked for a password.

WHAT ARE PRIMARY SOURCES?

Dear Everybody,

I'm looking forward to seeing you again, but I'm in no hurry to see the expressions on your faces when you see me. I want to see you try to hide the shock on your faces. You might even ask me for proof I'm your son. Don't feel bad. I see it in my own face every day.

—Private Al Puntasecca, in a letter to his family.

The soldier who wrote these words never dreamed that they would be read by anyone but his family. They were not intended to be read as a history of the Korean War. But his words—and the words of others that have come down to us through scholars or were saved over generations by family members—are unique resources. Historians call such writings primary source documents. As you read this book, you will find other primary source accounts of the war written by the men and women who fought it. Their letters home reflect their thoughts, their dreams, their fears, and their longing for loved ones. Some of them speak of the excitement of battle, while others mention the everyday boredom of day-to-day life in camp.

But the story of a war is not only the story of the men and women in service. This book also contains diary entries, newspaper accounts, official documents, and speeches of the war years. They reflect the opinions of those who were not in battle but who were still affected by the war. All of these things as well as photographs and art are primary sources—they were created by people who participated in, witnessed, or were affected by the events of the time.

Many of these sources, such as letters and diaries, are a reflection of personal experience. Others, such as newspaper accounts, reflect the mood of the time as well as the opinions of the papers' editors. All of them give us a unique insight into history as it happened. But it is also important to keep in mind that each source reflects its author's biases, beliefs, and background. Each is still someone's interpretation of an event.

Some of the primary sources in this book will be easy to understand; others may not. Their authors came from a different time and were products of different backgrounds and levels of education. So as you read their words, you will see that some of those words may be spelled differently than we would spell them. And some of their stories may be written without the kinds of punctuation we are used to seeing. Each source has been presented as it was originally written, but wherever a word or phrase is unclear or might be misunderstood, an explanation has been added.

TIME LINE OF THE KOREAN WAR

1945 —AUGUST 15: Japan surrenders, ending World War II, and is forced from Korea. Korea is divided into two zones at the 38th parallel. The Soviets control the northern part of the country, and the Americans control the southern part.

1948 —Two governments are in place: the Republic of Korea in the South, also called South Korea, and the Democratic People's Republic of Korea under Communist rule in the North, known as North Korea.

**mid-
1949** —Soviet and United States troops leave Korea.

1950 —JUNE 25: North Korea invades South Korea.

—JULY 7: The United Nations Security Council acts to create the United Nations Command, UNC, headed by General Douglas MacArthur.

—AUGUST 1: The battles around the Pusan Perimeter commence.

—SEPTEMBER 15: Inchon landings.

—OCTOBER 7: United Nations Command forces cross the 38th parallel.

—OCTOBER 14: First Phase Offensive: China enters the war. Chinese Communist forces begin crossing the Yalu River and attack South Korean forces.

—OCTOBER 15: President Harry S Truman and General Douglas MacArthur meet on Wake Island.

—NOVEMBER 24: Second Phase Offensive begins.

—NOVEMBER 27: Beginning of the Battle of Chosin Reservoir.

—DECEMBER 31: Third Phase Offensive begins.

1951 —JANUARY 25: Operation Thunderbolt recovers lost territory for UNC.

—FEBRUARY 11: Fourth Phase Offensive begins.

—APRIL 11: General MacArthur is dismissed. He is replaced by General Matthew Ridgway as commander of the UNC.

—APRIL 22: Fifth Phase Offensive begins.

—JUNE 23: The Soviets propose opening cease-fire negotiations.

—JULY 10: Negotiations for a cease-fire begin in Kaesong.

—AUGUST 23: The Communist delegation suspends cease-fire talks.

—OCTOBER 3: Operation Commando.

—OCTOBER 25: Cease-fire talks resume at Panmunjom.

1952 —MAY 7: Prisoners at Koje-do stage uprising and hold UNC prison commandant General Francis Dodd prisoner.

—MAY 12: General Mark Clark succeeds General Matthew Ridgway as commander of the UNC.

—JUNE 23: UNC air strikes against North Korean hydroelectric plants begin.

—JULY 11: First bombing of Pyongyang.

—AUGUST 29: Second bombing of Pyongyang.

—OCTOBER 8: UNC suspends cease-fire negotiations.

—NOVEMBER 4: Dwight D. Eisenhower is elected president of the United States.

1953 —MARCH 5: Soviet dictator Joseph Stalin dies.

—MARCH 23–24: Old Baldy and Pork Chop hills held by 31st Infantry Regiment of the U.S. 7th Infantry Division.

—APRIL 16–18: Battle of Pork Chop Hill; 17th and 31st Infantry units suffer heavy casualties.

—APRIL 26: Cease-fire negotiations resume in Panmunjom.

—MAY 13: UNC air strikes against North Korean dams commence.

—JUNE 10: Battle of the Kumsong Bulge.

—JUNE 16: First cease-fire.

—JUNE 18: South Korea protests the cease-fire.

—JULY 6–10: Final battle at Pork Chop Hill.

—JULY 13: Final Communist offensive.

—JULY 27: The United Nations, North Korea, and China sign an armistice, ending the fighting. South Korea refuses to sign.

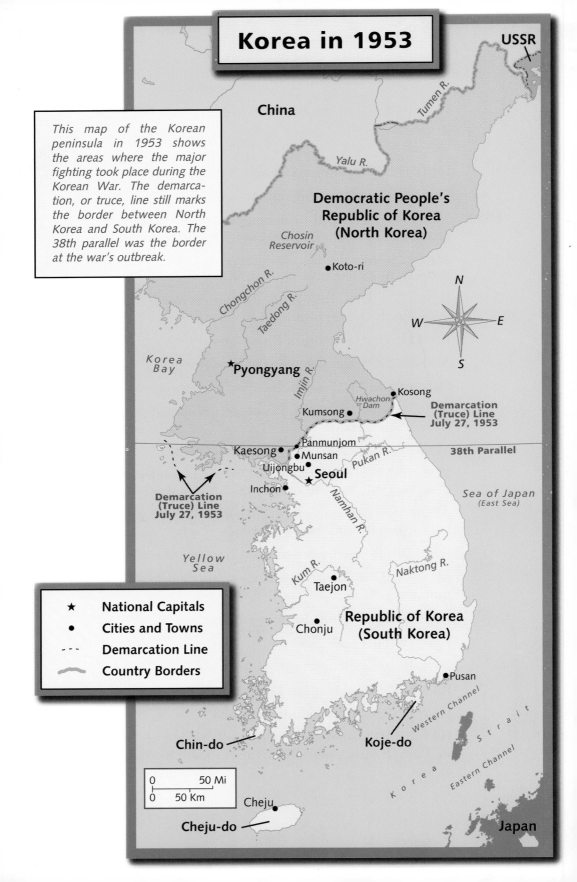

Korea in 1953

USSR

China

Tumen R.

Yalu R.

Democratic People's Republic of Korea (North Korea)

Chosin Reservoir

● Koto-ri

This map of the Korean peninsula in 1953 shows the areas where the major fighting took place during the Korean War. The demarcation, or truce, line still marks the border between North Korea and South Korea. The 38th parallel was the border at the war's outbreak.

Chongchon R.

Taedong R.

N

W   E

S

Korea Bay

★ **Pyongyang**

Imjin R.

Hwachon Dam   ● Kosong

Kumsong ●

Demarcation (Truce) Line July 27, 1953

Kaesong ●   ● Panmunjom

● Munsan

Pukan R.

38th Parallel

Uijongbu ●

★ **Seoul**

Inchon ●

Demarcation (Truce) Line July 27, 1953

Namhan R.

Sea of Japan (East Sea)

Yellow Sea

Kum R.

Naktong R.

Taejon ●

Chonju ●

Republic of Korea (South Korea)

● Pusan

★ **National Capitals**

● **Cities and Towns**

- - - **Demarcation Line**

〜 **Country Borders**

Western Channel

Chin-do

Koje-do

Korea Strait

Eastern Channel

0	50 Mi
0	50 Km

Cheju ●

Cheju-do

Japan

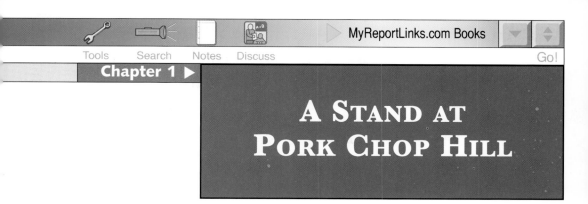
A STAND AT PORK CHOP HILL

Pork Chop Hill, or Hill 255, as it was officially known, was a United Nations military outpost in western Korea along the 38th parallel, the line that divided the Democratic People's Republic of Korea from the Republic of Korea. The Korean War began in 1950 when Communist forces from the North

▲ Sergeant Martin Lorenz, 7th Infantry Division, left, and another American soldier stand on Pork Chop Hill in 1953.

crossed that line and invaded the South. The war eventually involved North Korea and Communist China on one side and a coalition of forces, including those of the United States, which made up the United Nations Command (UNC), on the other side.

In the spring of 1953, the war had been raging for nearly three long years. The final battles for Pork Chop Hill, which began in March and ended in July, marked the longest continual struggle on a single battlefield of that war. The battle to save Pork Chop resulted in heavy casualties to United Nations troops who held the hill against overwhelming enemy forces, claiming the lives of American soldiers as well as the lives of soldiers from Thailand, Colombia, and South Korea.

▶ A Back-and-Forth Struggle

The action at Pork Chop was typical of the seesaw battles that marked the latter half of the Korean War. Each side tried to cause as many casualties to the other as possible while keeping damage to their own forces to a minimum. Each hoped that the costs of the war would be too much for the other to bear and would bring the enemy to the negotiating table. Both the United Nations and Communist forces adopted these tactics to seize the upper hand in the cease-fire negotiations that had been going on since 1951.

Pork Chop Hill was the sight of fighting on March 23 and 24 and again on April 16 through 18. Despite repeated attacks by the Chinese and North Koreans,

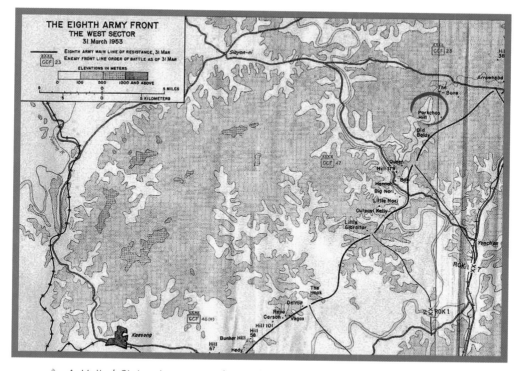

▲ A United States Army map shows the main line of resistance of the west sector of the Eighth Army in March 1953. Hill 255, Pork Chop, is highlighted.

the American forces held the hill. At first, Pork Chop Hill, held by the U.S. Army 7th Infantry Division, operated in a quieter part of the Main Line of Resistance (MLR), the front line of combat. The war seemed to be coming to a close. There already had been an exchange of wounded prisoners of war.

U.S. Army Infantry Lieutenant Dick Shea wrote a letter to his wife, Joyce, during one of the quiet moments of June 22, 1953:

I have a few moments, then I must clean my weapon, and perhaps tomorrow, rather tonight I mean, I will have some more time to write. At present I'm in my sandbag command post (similar to one of those in the watercolor) at the base of a cliff.[1]

There were rumors of a truce or cease-fire, but the war crept on through the sea of mud that was the Korean spring and early summer of 1953. The soldiers hoped that the negotiations in Panmunjom, a village on the border, would end soon so that they could go home. Still, the Chinese and North Korean forces kept up the pressure on the front lines to gain more leverage at the negotiating table. They also were trying to save face, since the Communist government had conceded, or given in to, nearly every major demand of the United Nations by the middle of 1953. In Asian cultures, saving face is an important concept, having more to do with retaining the honor of a group or family structure than keeping one's own pride intact.

On Pork Chop Hill, the Communist forces still seemed a distant if ever-present threat in the summer of 1953. Dick Shea wrote to his wife again, on June 29:

We had been behind hill 200 all night, the artillery thundered and flashed, and flares lit up the sky and valley, but the incoming was elsewhere and we slept sound, though chilly, under a sky that held no rain for us this night at least. But the creeks and streams are swollen and swift. The monsoon season is upon us, and everywhere the roads and trails turn to mud, then knee deep soup. Yesterday our vehicles began using snow chains to combat the mud. Going to the bivouac area where our company is quartered, Scotty, the driver, drove his jeep along the stream bed, which was a smoother, better road than the oozing earth on the bank above. Last night as we were to move at seven, I went ahead with a small detail of men, two jeeps and trailer, to build a foot bridge across the now raging torrent of the bubbling little stream I have described to you, behind 200. As the men pulled back yesterday at dawn, they had to wade knee deep in water, and we did not want them to get wet clothing and boots and have to sleep out in them all night.[2]

Renewed Attacks

By July 6, however, the Communist assault began, and the fighting was brutal as the battle seesawed back and forth. Each side captured ground and then lost it in a series of relentless attacks. John Phillips, a private in the newly arrived George Company of the 17th Infantry, recalled the action.

As each soldier, squad, or small group filed up the trench to the bunker and the line of departure, he checked that we did a lock-and-load on personal weapons. (With all the yelling, noise, artillery bursts, and small arms snapping around, troops can get so nervous that they forget to load their weapons.) The sergeant could glance out the bunker aperture at the troops who had gone before, so he could regulate the pace. The sergeant reminded each soldier to keep his head down, to maintain the standard, combat zone, five-yard separation, and to keep moving to the top of Pork Chop. Maybe five or six wounded were inside the bunker and on litters [stretchers] in the adjacent trench awaiting evacuation, and a medic was working among them.

Suddenly it was World War I all over again. At the sergeant's signal, each person put his right foot on the firing step, swung his left leg up and over, and clamored out of the trench outside the bunker, over the top, and started down the slope toward Pork Chop. No one had any idea what was over the top or down the slope or what had happened to those who preceded him. For all we knew a Chinese machine gun was cutting down everyone on the path. All we knew was that when your turn came, you went.[3]

By likening the action to "World War I all over again," Phillips was referring to the bloody trench warfare that characterized the First World War. In Korea, thirty-five years later, the same kind of fighting was happening. Phillips went on to describe what he saw in the trenches:

In one long section the bottom of the trench was so littered with bodies that in many places they were several deep. We had no time to move them and no place to which to move them. You had to step on them to move forward. I do not know whether the dead were already there when George Company arrived or whether they were from the lead elements of George Company. Chinese could have been among them. They were the first battlefield dead I had been close to. I tried not to look at them, but you could not walk on them without looking at them. We all resembled each other in age and dress. . . .[4]

Angel Palermo was a twenty-one-year-old private in Able Company, 17th Infantry. He recalled the brutal hand-to-hand combat of the final battle for Pork Chop Hill:

The Chinese were on their loudspeakers telling us to surrender. If we did not, they said, we were all going to die. They announced that they were going to take Porkchop and that they would take no prisoners. On the night of July 6, as it started to get dark, the Chinese attacked in force. I was on a .50-caliber machine gun when they started to swarm up the hill. I could have sworn that all of China was on that slope. With enough firepower, we could have killed a thousand gooks [an insulting term for the Chinese or North Koreans], but

▲ *Sergeant Lorenz stands in his bunker on Hill 255 "before all hell broke loose," in his words.*

we hadn't nearly enough ammunition to turn back this kind of attack. We fired the .50 until we ran out of ammo, and by that time the Chinese were in our trenchline, so we fought them with rifle butts, bayonets, and even fists and helmets. They were pushing us back, but before we were driven off the hill, Baker Company came up to help us. However, the sheer numbers of Chinese drove us off the top of Porkchop.[5]

On July 10, after five days of relentless attacks by the enemy, the Americans fighting on Pork Chop Hill were given the order to evacuate. When the war finally ended with the signing of an armistice only a few weeks later, Pork Chop Hill became part of the demilitarized zone (DMZ) dividing the Koreas. It also came to symbolize the futility of the war itself, with both sides inflicting heavy casualties upon the other and no territory gained or victor declared.

For the families of American servicemen such as Dick Shea, however, it marked the ultimate sacrifice. Unfortunately, too many families in the United States received letters about lost loved ones.

Korea
August 31, 1953
Dear Mrs. Shea,
    I hope that I am not reopening old wounds but I would like to write to you about Dick. I was his Battalion Commander on Pork Chop and can give you some factual information which you may not have.
    In the early attacks by the Chinese he led to my personal knowledge five counterattacks. In one of them he received a slight wound on the cheek. He

gave me much valuable information all during the action. . . . I received orders that the remainder of my battalion would be relieved and replaced by a new unit. There were about 25 A Company men in the right sector. Dick's job was to keep these men together and to leave the hill with them. I personally covered his run to this action with rifle fire—he made it safely. Shortly thereafter the new unit attacked—my people were being withdrawn. One of the platoons of the new unit suffered casualties among its officers and non commissioned officers. Dick saw their confusion and carefully turned the remaining men of "A" Company over to another man, reorganized the troops from the other unit and personally led them in an attack in which he was killed. The battle continued and the ground was taken and retaken many times. Dick's action was beyond the call of duty in many respects. First, he took command of other troops than his own, he could have evacuated himself, or he could have simply held the disorganized men under cover. As you know any action other than the action he took would not have been characteristic of him. His action saved lives because the people he took were lost without his leadership.

He was clearly the most outstanding officer of his grade I have served with. He was recommended for the Medal of Honor because we his comrades know he earned it and we loved him.

He used to kid me about being too old to keep up with him—my father was track coach at VMI [Virginia Military Institute] for 30 years and I ran (poorly). I am from Lexington, Virginia and he did say that Virginians should stick together and not let the wall Korea builds separate them. At 33, not 23, it was a job keeping up with him. I have two sons and I hope that someday they will show the same sense of honor and duty that your husband displayed.

He was much more to me than a young rifle platoon leader. His life will be a constant inspiration to me and I shall be a better man for having known him.

An injured chaplain offers a memorial to Marines killed near Koto-ri, Korea, December 3, 1950. Nearly 34,000 Americans were killed in the Korean War.

▲ This photograph of Pork Chop Hill as seen from above was supplied by Sergeant Martin Lorenz, who survived the war and returned to New York.

Sergeant Lorenz, right, and Sergeant ▷ Betenball were the only ones left from their original company at war's end.

My heart is too full to say more and I'm sorry I can't express what I feel.

May God bless you.

BM Read
Lt Colonel
Infantry
17th Inf Regiment[6]

A BRIEF HISTORY
OF THE
KOREAN WAR

Korea, a peninsula in Southeast Asia once home to ancient kingdoms and a united people, was ruled by the Japanese from 1905 until August 1945. Throughout this period, the Korean people wanted to become an independent country again, but Korea's people disagreed about how that should be achieved. Two groups emerged. One was the Nationalist government that lived in exile abroad,

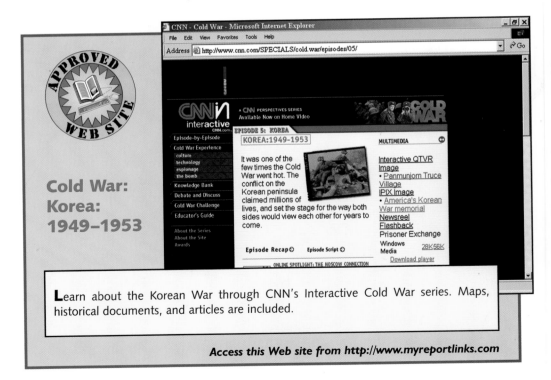

Cold War: Korea: 1949–1953

Learn about the Korean War through CNN's Interactive Cold War series. Maps, historical documents, and articles are included.

Access this Web site from http://www.myreportlinks.com

first in Shanghai in China and then in the United States during the Second World War. The other group was composed of the Communist guerrilla fighters who fought the Japanese during the war and received support from the Soviet Union, the world's largest Communist power.[1]

A Divided Country

The Japanese surrender on August 15, 1945, opened the door for Korea's independence. The victorious Allies had determined before the war ended that Korea should be ruled by an international trustee-ship. However, Soviet armies seized North Korea before the armistice, and the United States military decided that it would need to occupy the southern part of Korea. Finally, the Soviet Union and the United States agreed to divide the Korean peninsula along the 38th parallel until a settlement regarding the Korean government could be reached.[2]

Following World War II, the United States sup-ported the Nationalist government, preparing it to take the reins of power in Korea eventually. At the same time, the Soviets groomed the North Korean Communist party to take over.

In December 1945, the United States and the Soviet Union came to an agreement at the Moscow Conference on how a Korean government should be formed.[3] But most South Korean political parties refused to recognize the agreement and were thus disqualified from holding political office in Korea.

With South Korea not participating in 1947, the United States decided to turn the problem over to the United Nations, or UN, the global organization formed in 1945 to maintain international peace and security among the world's countries.

The United Nations Becomes Involved

The UN then set up the United Nations Temporary Commission on Korea, or UNTCOK, to supervise the election of an assembly that would determine Korea's government before American and Soviet troops were withdrawn from Korea. The Soviets objected to UNTCOK and did not allow UNTCOK officials into North Korea, so UNTCOK held elections in South Korea to determine a national government.[4]

National Archives: The United States Enters the Korean Conflict

This Web page of the National Archives and Records Administration features a brief overview of the Korean War and presents President Truman's proclamation of June 27, 1950, committing American forces to fight in Korea.

Access this Web site from http://www.myreportlinks.com

On May 10, 1948, the Korean elections were held, but they were marred by widespread corruption, fraud, and violence. Dr. Syngman Rhee and his government in exile secured the majority of seats in the assembly, and Rhee was elected president of Korea.[5] The United Nations General Assembly recognized the new Korean government, but the Soviets blocked Korea's admission to the United Nations through their veto in the Security Council.[6] The Soviet Union, as one of the five permanent members of the Security Council, had the power to veto any new members or actions by the UN.

The Soviets held their own elections in North Korea, and a Communist government was set up with Kim Il Sung as the premier. The Korean peninsula was now home to two governments, each claiming to be the legitimate one for the entire country.

▶ Fighting Begins

In 1945, with the end of World War II, a guerrilla war erupted in the Korean countryside between groups that supported the Communists and those that supported the Nationalists. In the beginning, it consisted of raids and skirmishes, but by April 1948, fighting exploded on the island of Cheju-do. The police sent to put down the rebellion joined it instead. President Rhee and his government resorted to harsh methods to put down the fighting. By January 1949, nearly thirty thousand people had been killed.[7]

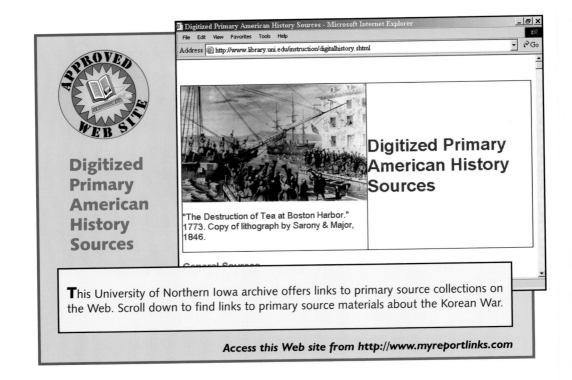

Digitized Primary American History Sources - Microsoft Internet Explorer

File   Edit   View   Favorites   Tools   Help

Address http://www.library.uni.edu/instruction/digitalhistory.shtml   Go

Digitized Primary American History Sources

"The Destruction of Tea at Boston Harbor." 1773. Copy of lithograph by Sarony & Major, 1846.

APPROVED WEB SITE

Digitized Primary American History Sources

This University of Northern Iowa archive offers links to primary source collections on the Web. Scroll down to find links to primary source materials about the Korean War.

Access this Web site from http://www.myreportlinks.com

▷ The Rise of Communist China

At the same time that Korea was torn by fighting, its large neighbor to the north, China, was torn apart by civil war between Communists led by Mao Zedong and Nationalists led by Chiang Kai-shek. The Communists seized the mainland of China while the Nationalist government fled to the island of Taiwan in 1949.[8] Mao Zedong was interested in protecting his new government from what he believed was American imperialism, since the United States was the only significant world power in the Pacific after World War II. While the Chinese Communist party had differences with the Soviets, Mao Zedong decided that it was in China's interest to "lean to one side." Chairman Mao allied his nation with the Soviet Union to secure development and military aid to rebuild China. The two Communist powers also had a mutual interest in checking American influence in the Far East.[9]

The Soviet Involvement

Kim Il Sung asked Joseph Stalin, the Soviet Union's leader, to lend his support for a military invasion of South Korea to unify the country under one Communist government. At first, Stalin was reluctant to make a move toward a war that might include the United States. However, by the end of 1949, Stalin changed his mind.[10] The Soviets had recently exploded their own atomic bomb, and the

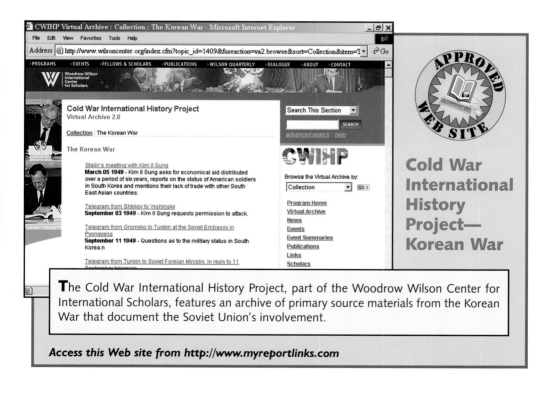

The Cold War International History Project, part of the Woodrow Wilson Center for International Scholars, features an archive of primary source materials from the Korean War that document the Soviet Union's involvement.

Access this Web site from http://www.myreportlinks.com

threat that the United States might use atomic weapons against the Soviet Union concerned Stalin. Also, the Communist victory in the Chinese civil war meant that there was more Communist influence in the Far East than had existed before. Finally, it was thought that Korea was not important to United States' interests. Stalin also wanted to act before Japan, a country influenced by the United States, could recover its economic and military power. By helping to establish a Communist government in Korea, the Soviet Union could keep the United States from gaining a foothold in mainland East Asia. That would create tensions between the United States and the Communist government in China.[11]

In April 1950, Stalin consented to Kim Il Sung's requests and approved an invasion of South Korea after receiving assurances from the North Korean leader that North Korea's army could defeat the South Koreans in a few weeks, long before the United States could become involved.[12]

The War Begins

On June 25, 1950, the armies of North Korea crossed the 38th parallel and invaded South Korea. The invasion shocked South Korea, known as the Republic of Korea, or ROK, and the United States.

The attack was viewed by the American government as a direct assault on United States' interests. It was seen as a test of the United States' resolve to stand up to Communist aggression. The invasion was

President Harry S Truman signed a proclamation on December 16, 1950, declaring a national emergency following China's entry in the Korean War.

also seen as a security threat to Japan, which was viewed as an important future United States ally.

Harry S Truman, the United States president, decided to bring the issue to the UN Security Council. With the Soviet Union boycotting the UN over the issue of which Chinese government, Communist or Nationalist, should be seated in the Security Council, its absence allowed the United States and its allies in the UN to pass a series of resolutions. The resolutions condemned the North Korean invasion of South Korea; created a United Nations Command, the UNC; and appointed General Douglas MacArthur of the U.S. Army as its commander to use military force to defend South Korea. As many as seventeen countries contributed troops to the effort, though the United States and the Republic of Korea supplied the greatest number of troops and material to the war effort.[13]

▶ A War in Phases

The Korean War can be divided into two distinct phases: a war of maneuver and a war of attrition, or weakening by persistent attack. The early part of the war was fought by each side moving large numbers of troops up and down the Korean peninsula with the goal of achieving a "total victory," a decisive defeat of the enemy. Later, the idea of total victory was abandoned, first by the UNC and later by the Communists. When it became clear that the war could not be won without it intensifying—involving more countries and possibly the use of atomic weapons, which would kill millions—both sides opted to fight a war of attrition. The strategy caused many more casualties and made it so expensive for the enemy to fight that it would negotiate a settlement. This aim for a settlement is also known as a limited war because it seeks limited goals for the victor and it also limits what one side or the other is willing to do to win the war.[14]

▷ The North's Early Advance

Early in the war, both sides had the unification of Korea under a single government as their goal. That had been the reason for the North Korean invasion. The North Korean troops were better trained and

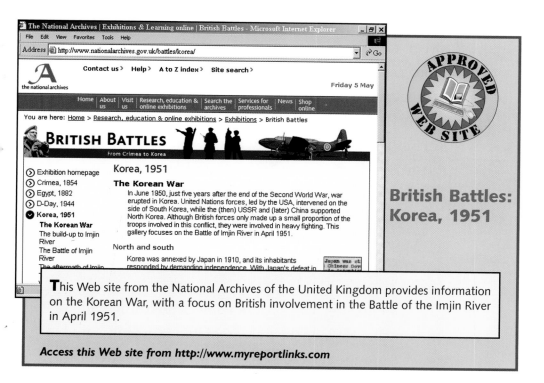

British Battles: Korea, 1951

This Web site from the National Archives of the United Kingdom provides information on the Korean War, with a focus on British involvement in the Battle of the Imjin River in April 1951.

Access this Web site from http://www.myreportlinks.com

better equipped than their South Korean opponents, and they were more experienced because many of them had just fought in China's civil war. The North Korean forces quickly overran most of South Korea.

In a matter of weeks, they managed to push the South Korean armed forces and the small number of American forces into the far southeastern corner of the Korean peninsula, an area known as the Pusan Perimeter. It was so named because it was a defensive position located around the port city of Pusan. The United States and British navies moved quickly to blockade the Korean peninsula. That gave the UNC an advantage since the North Korean military had a small fleet. The UNC fleets used aircraft launched from carriers to conduct air strikes on North Korean troops and positions. They quickly swept the North Korean Air Force from the skies, protecting the ground troops trapped in the Pusan Perimeter.[15]

The United States ferried reinforcements to the Korean peninsula as rapidly as possible to slow the tide of the North Korean invasion and protect Pusan. Finally, the North Korean assaults were thrown back with heavy casualties, and the battle line stabilized into a siege of the area around Pusan.

▶ MacArthur's Strategy

UNC commander General Douglas MacArthur had other plans. He launched an amphibious assault, an attack from the sea onto land, at Inchon, a port city

▲ *General Douglas MacArthur, with other officers, watches the shelling of Inchon from the USS* Mount McKinley *on September 15, 1950.*

on the west coast of Korea. His aim was to cut off the North Korean Army's communications and supply lines and devastate the North Korean forces with one quick attack.[16] Inchon was also selected as the landing point because with its rugged terrain, the enemy would not consider it a landing place and not bother to defend it. The Inchon landing proved to be an act of military genius on MacArthur's part.

▶ The Marines Land and the Tide Turns

On September 15, 1950, Admiral Arthur Dewey Struble, a decorated World War II veteran, commanded the 261 Navy ships that landed 80,000

Marines through the shifting tides at Inchon in the first wave of the assault. The defending North Koreans put up little resistance, retreating to Seoul, the South Korean capital. The battle for Seoul was difficult, but the UNC troops finally prevailed. This invasion allowed the UNC forces trapped in the Pusan Perimeter to break out, and the North Korean Army was virtually destroyed. It was a stunning reversal of fortune, swinging the war in favor of the South Koreans.[17] The victory, however, seemed so complete and total that it threatened both the Soviet and Chinese governments, who had a strong interest in keeping North Korea Communist.[18]

North Korea Gets Help

Ever since American troops became involved in the war, the Communist Chinese, in particular, felt threatened by the presence of American soldiers so near. There was concern that without a buffer, the United States would have a strategic base to invade Manchuria, China's most important industrial province, which lay just across the Korean border. After meeting with other Chinese Communist leaders, Mao Zedong decided it was time to become involved. He agreed to send a portion of the Chinese Army, designated the Chinese People's Volunteers, or CPV, to help North Korea and remove UNC forces from the Korean peninsula once and for all. Joseph Stalin and the Soviets offered military aid in the form of munitions as well as limited air support in the form of planes and pilots, though these were carefully painted and uniformed as Chinese or North Korean and not Soviet.[19] Stalin wanted to be careful to avoid a direct confrontation with the United States, which could quickly turn into a third world war.

MacArthur's Advance North

As UNC troops approached the 38th parallel, the Chinese issued warnings to the UNC that they would

United Nations ground forces first crossed the 38th parallel into North Korea in October 1950 but were forced back into South Korea by Chinese troops.

not accept UNC soldiers moving any closer to the Chinese border. General MacArthur, who knew he had the North Korean Army defeated, and President Truman, whose advisors felt that the warnings were not serious, elected to pursue the North Korean Army. The UNC troops crossed the 38th parallel in the first week of October 1950.[20] President Truman, concerned with the consequences of ignoring the Chinese warning, met with General MacArthur on Wake Island, in the central Pacific Ocean. MacArthur convinced his Commander in Chief that there were no signs of either China or the Soviet Union planning to retaliate. The United Nations backed the plan to unify Korea under the Republic of Korea's government and approved MacArthur's advance across the 38th parallel.

The First Phase Offensive

While not as well equipped as the North Korean forces, the Chinese forces included soldiers who had fought in World War II and the Chinese civil war. They were tough and hardy veteran troops.[21] On October 14, 1950, they crossed the Yalu River, the border between China and Korea, and attacked South Korean troops in an overwhelming assault known as the First Phase Offensive.[22] After defeating the South Koreans, the CPV then took up defensive positions. They were taking advantage of the UNC's over-extended supply and communications lines and the mountainous terrain of North Korea. Unsure of

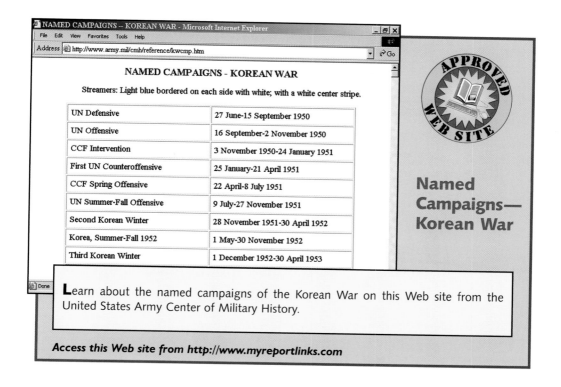

NAMED CAMPAIGNS -- KOREAN WAR - Microsoft Internet Explorer

File   Edit   View   Favorites   Tools   Help

Address http://www.army.mil/cmh/reference/kwcmp.htm   Go

NAMED CAMPAIGNS - KOREAN WAR

Streamers: Light blue bordered on each side with white; with a white center stripe.

UN Defensive	27 June-15 September 1950
UN Offensive	16 September-2 November 1950
CCF Intervention	3 November 1950-24 January 1951
First UN Counteroffensive	25 January-21 April 1951
CCF Spring Offensive	22 April-8 July 1951
UN Summer-Fall Offensive	9 July-27 November 1951
Second Korean Winter	28 November 1951-30 April 1952
Korea, Summer-Fall 1952	1 May-30 November 1952
Third Korean Winter	1 December 1952-30 April 1953

Named Campaigns— Korean War

Done

Learn about the named campaigns of the Korean War on this Web site from the United States Army Center of Military History.

Access this Web site from http://www.myreportlinks.com

exactly what happened, General MacArthur ordered the advance to continue, but many UNC troops felt the war was all but won and the advance was ill conceived and reckless.[23]

The Second Phase Offensive

On November 24, 1950, MacArthur's decision led UNC troops into a trap by the CPV in what was called the Second Phase Offensive. CPV units moved off road to encircle and trap the UNC units, hoping to overwhelm them with greater numbers. The offensive was nearly successful; the South Korean forces were hit hard, and the 2nd U.S. Infantry Division was nearly surrounded. The rest of the U.S. Army quickly pulled back as the 2nd Division fought its way through intense enemy small-arms fire to safety. The 2nd Division would have suffered a worse fate if the CPV had better artillery. Without it, they were unable to completely block the 2nd Division's escape route.[24]

▷ The "Frozen Chosin"

Elsewhere, the CPV made an attack on UNC forces approaching the Yalu River near the Chosin Reservoir. The attack surrounded the 5th and 7th U.S. Marine regiments. The Marines inflicted heavy casualties on the frontal assaults of the CPV and managed to work

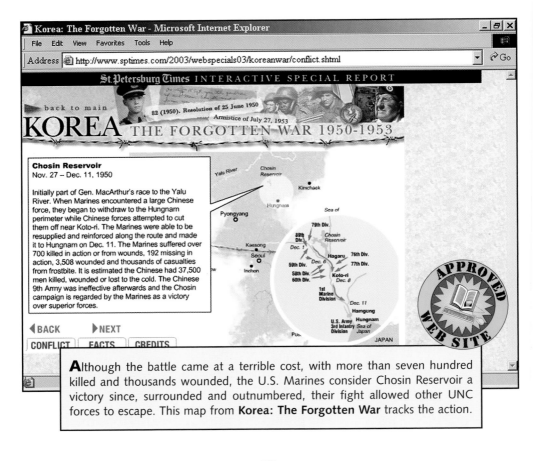

Although the battle came at a terrible cost, with more than seven hundred killed and thousands wounded, the U.S. Marines consider Chosin Reservoir a victory since, surrounded and outnumbered, their fight allowed other UNC forces to escape. This map from **Korea: The Forgotten War** tracks the action.

a breakout from their positions while suffering nearly forty-four hundred casualties themselves. But these Marine regiments so easily handled the CPV's Ninth Army Corps that it had to return to China to regroup.[25] Major General O. P. Smith, commander of the U.S. Marines in Korea, was quoted as saying, "Retreat, hell—we're attacking in another direction."[26] The Marines' action gave the UNC time to move back to the 38th parallel. The retreat from the Yalu River became the longest retreat in United States military history.[27] The Marines who fought at the Frozen Chosin, their nickname for the fight, did not consider it a retreat but a victory as they battled both overwhelming enemy forces and overwhelmingly cold temperatures.

Change to Limited War

The embarrassing rout of the UNC forces by the CPV threw UNC headquarters into chaos. Many officers, including General MacArthur, wanted to escalate the conflict to retaliate against Communist China. Neither the leaders of the United States nor those of the other countries in the United Nations Command, however, wanted to do that. President Truman and Prime Minister Clement Attlee of Great Britain agreed to fight a limited war. Their goal was to bring the Communists to the bargaining table to reach a diplomatic settlement to the Korean War.[28]

General MacArthur's orders were to abandon plans for a decisive victory in Korea, but instead he

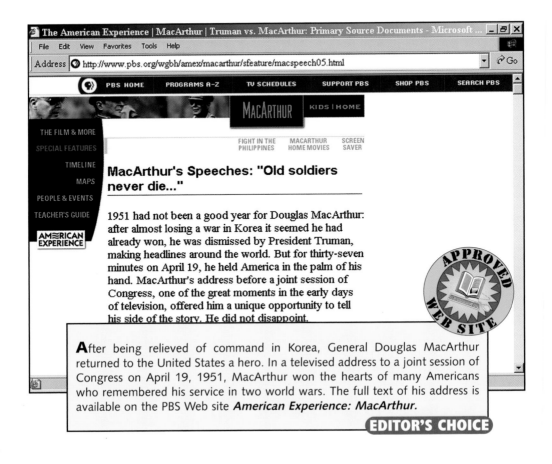

The American Experience | MacArthur | Truman vs. MacArthur: Primary Source Documents - Microsoft ...

File   Edit   View   Favorites   Tools   Help

Address   http://www.pbs.org/wgbh/amex/macarthur/sfeature/macspeech05.html   Go

PBS HOME   PROGRAMS A-Z   TV SCHEDULES   SUPPORT PBS   SHOP PBS   SEARCH PBS

MACARTHUR   KIDS I HOME

FIGHT IN THE   MACARTHUR   SCREEN
PHILIPPINES   HOME MOVIES   SAVER

THE FILM & MORE
SPECIAL FEATURES
TIMELINE
MAPS
PEOPLE & EVENTS
TEACHER'S GUIDE
AMERICAN
EXPERIENCE

MacArthur's Speeches: "Old soldiers never die..."

1951 had not been a good year for Douglas MacArthur:
after almost losing a war in Korea it seemed he had
already won, he was dismissed by President Truman,
making headlines around the world. But for thirty-seven
minutes on April 19, he held America in the palm of his
hand. MacArthur's address before a joint session of
Congress, one of the great moments in the early days
of television, offered him a unique opportunity to tell
his side of the story. He did not disappoint.

After being relieved of command in Korea, General Douglas MacArthur
returned to the United States a hero. In a televised address to a joint session of
Congress on April 19, 1951, MacArthur won the hearts of many Americans
who remembered his service in two world wars. The full text of his address is
available on the PBS Web site *American Experience: MacArthur.*

EDITOR'S CHOICE

came up with plans for blockades and air assaults on
Communist China, including an attack from Taiwan
to serve as a diversion.[29] His plan was rejected
because the leaders of the United States and those of
the countries in the United Nations forces wanted to
avoid any action that might bring the Soviet Union
into the fight directly.

More Offensives and Operation Thunderbolt

The U.S. Army's strategy focused on conserving
manpower and inflicting as much damage on the

enemy as possible. When the Chinese and North Koreans launched the Third Phase Offensive on December 31, 1950, UNC forces withstood the assault and countered with their own attack. Operation Thunderbolt, launched on January 25, 1951, recovered all the territory that the UNC had lost in their retreat from the Yalu.[30] Surprised at the UNC's success, the CPV launched the Fourth Phase Offensive. Although it was successful at first, the Chinese suffered heavy casualties. With those casualties and little gains in territory, the Communist forces adopted a strategy similar to the UNC's of avoiding battles to save men and material. That tactic enabled the UNC to push past the 38th parallel through brief attacks into more defensible

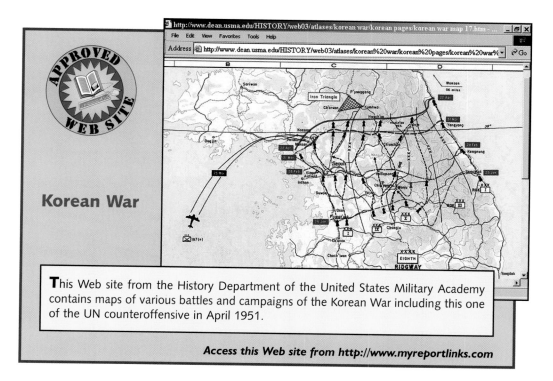

Korean War

This Web site from the History Department of the United States Military Academy contains maps of various battles and campaigns of the Korean War including this one of the UN counteroffensive in April 1951.

Access this Web site from http://www.myreportlinks.com

positions in the hills to the north. This position became known as the Kansas Line.[31]

MacArthur Is Replaced

General MacArthur, never comfortable fighting a limited war, saw Communist China as a serious threat. He used the media to argue for escalation and appealed to his friends in Congress. MacArthur also publicly criticized the Truman administration's policies on the war. On April 11, 1951, President Truman asked Douglas MacArthur to resign his command of the UNC forces.[32] Truman replaced MacArthur with General Matthew Ridgway, a brilliant officer who understood the tactics and strategies of fighting a limited war. As commanding officer of the U.S. Seventh Army in Korea, Ridgway had proven his ability as a leader.

The Fifth Phase Offensive

As the spring of 1951 approached, Communist forces prepared to launch a large-scale offensive hoping to recapture Seoul and Uijongbu. On April 22, 1951, the CPV launched the Fifth Phase Offensive.[33] After the Chinese forces broke through the South Korean units, the eastern portion of the assault was slowed by tough resistance from the 27th Commonwealth Brigade, made up of soldiers from Great Britain, Canada, Australia, and New Zealand. Another Communist force trying to capture Seoul was met by the 29th Commonwealth Brigade. The Gloucester

▲ When President Truman removed General MacArthur from command in Korea, many Americans were upset. The GI who erected these signs along a Korean highway in April 1951 also felt strongly about "Mac's" dismissal by "Harry" but found a humorous way to express himself.

Regiment bore the brunt of the assault and managed to hold back the Communist advance until April 25. Though that regiment suffered heavy casualties, its stand delayed the CPV's thrust enough to allow the rest of the UNC troops to recover. They were able to halt the offensive before the CPV reached Seoul. By

On May 18, 1952, as negotiations to end the fighting in Korea dragged on, President Truman expressed his frustration with the delays in a diary. On earlier pages, he accused the Communists in Korea of murdering prisoners of war and civilians. Here, he delivers an ultimatum to the enemy: End the hostilities in Korea or suffer the destruction of China and Siberia.

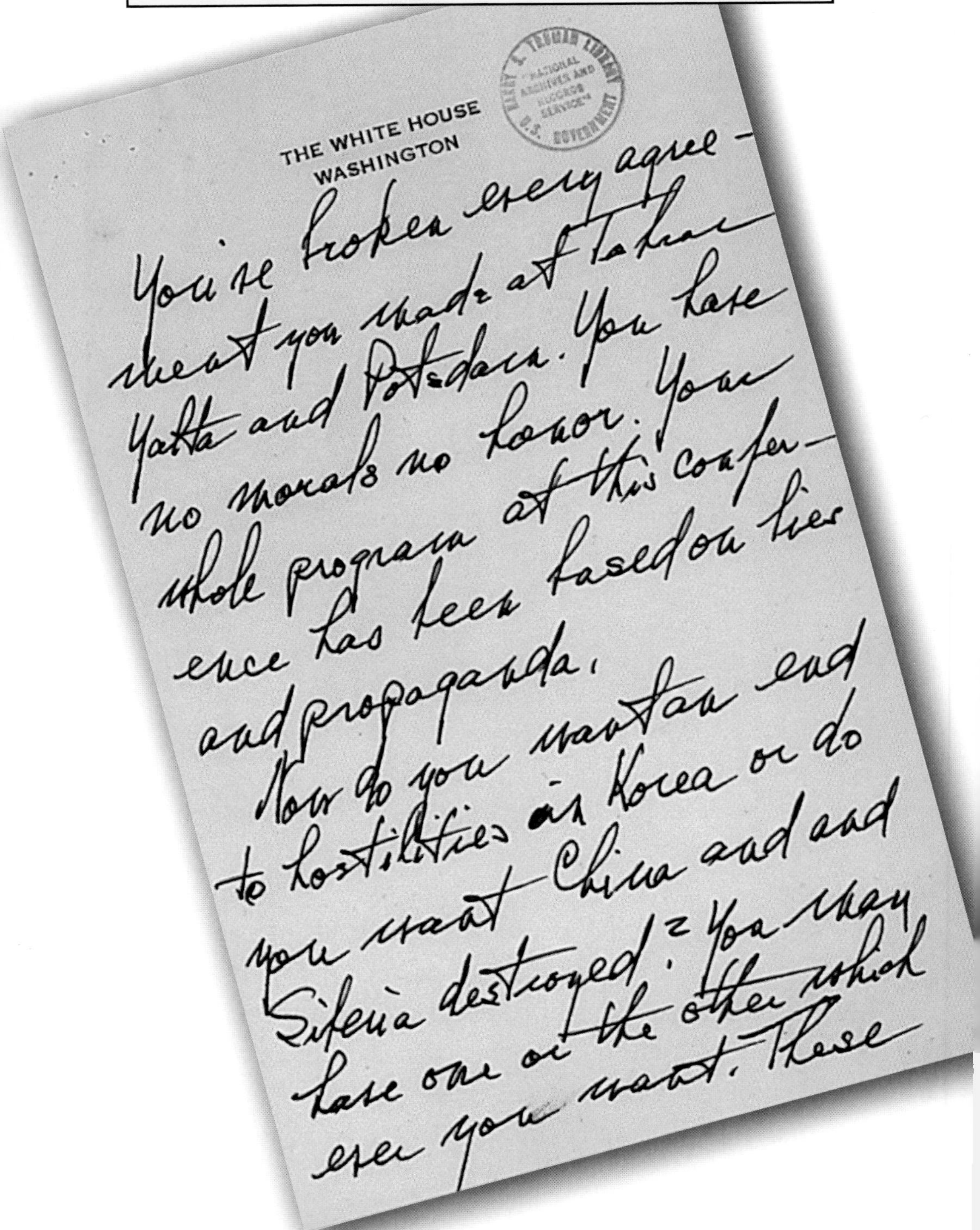

THE WHITE HOUSE
WASHINGTON

You've broken every agreement you made at Tehran
Yalta and Potsdam. You have
no morals no honor. Your
whole program at this conference has been based on lies
and propaganda.

Now do you want an end
to hostilities in Korea or do
you want China and and
Siberia destroyed? You may
have one or the other which
ever you want. These

late May, the offensive ground to a halt, and the UNC counterattacked and retook the Kansas Line.[34]

The Fifth Phase Offensive marked a turning point for the Chinese and North Koreans. It proved to the Chinese that the UNC forces could not be decisively defeated. The war was taking a heavy toll on the Chinese economy. Both China and the Soviet Union decided to negotiate a cease-fire. From this point forward, the war was fought with cease-fire negotiations in mind, and each side tried to strengthen its position at the bargaining table by its actions on the battlefield.

▶ Negotiations Begin

On July 10, 1951, the first official negotiations were held behind Communist lines at Kaesong. The talks were supposed to establish a cease-fire line, supervisory arrangements for the cease-fire, an exchange of prisoners, and eventually a political settlement of the war. But the fighting continued while the talks dragged on.

The Chinese command, believing it could wear down the UNC forces, adopted a strategy of small but repeated offensives to cause heavy UNC casualties. Even if the CPV casualties were greater, the Chinese had a larger troop supply than the UNC.

On August 23, 1951, the Communist delegation suspended negotiations, claiming UNC violations in the area around Kaesong.[35] Negotiations were already at a stalemate. The Communists wanted the cease-fire line at the 38th parallel, while the UNC wanted the line of contact, the Kansas Line, to act as the cease-fire line, since it offered better defensive positions.[36] General Ridgway's military action during the halt in negotiations was a series of more limited offensives to pressure the CPV into accepting the line of contact as the cease-fire line. The offensives pushed the CPV farther up the Korean peninsula.

When peace talks resumed at a different place, Panmunjom, the Chinese delegation gave in regarding the cease-fire line, but details over the supervision of the cease-fire and the return of prisoners remained areas of disagreement. For most of the later months of 1951 and the early months of 1952, both sides tried to cause as much damage to the other as possible, although the UNC shifted its strategy. It began an air campaign to bring about an advantage at the negotiating table.

▶ The Air War

The Korean War was the first war that featured the large-scale use of jets. The North Korean and Chinese forces used the Soviet-built MiG–15. The UNC forces relied primarily upon the F–86 Sabre, a plane that was faster and sturdier than the Soviet fighter but not as maneuverable. For most of the war, the UNC maintained air superiority over Korea, but the Communist forces were able to intercept the UNC's daylight bombing raids because the MiGs could operate at much higher altitudes.[37] The

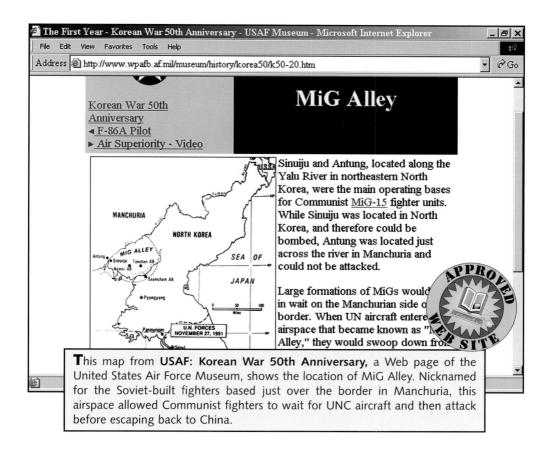

MiG Alley

Sinuiju and Antung, located along the Yalu River in northeastern North Korea, were the main operating bases for Communist MiG-15 fighter units. While Sinuiju was located in North Korea, and therefore could be bombed, Antung was located just across the river in Manchuria and could not be attacked.

Large formations of MiGs would in wait on the Manchurian side o border. When UN aircraft entere airspace that became known as " Alley," they would swoop down fro

This map from **USAF: Korean War 50th Anniversary,** a Web page of the United States Air Force Museum, shows the location of MiG Alley. Nicknamed for the Soviet-built fighters based just over the border in Manchuria, this airspace allowed Communist fighters to wait for UNC aircraft and then attack before escaping back to China.

Communist forces also controlled an area of north-western Korea known as MiG Alley because it lay close to the MiG air bases in China.

At first, UNC forces used that location to their advantage in trying to cut off supplies to the North Korean and CPV forces. But as the war became a fight of attrition, without much troop movement, supply trains became less crucial, and UNC bombers had fewer targets.[38] When the air blockade ceased to be successful, the UNC decided to change strategies again—at the same time that negotiations and the land war bogged down.

APPROVED WEB SITE

U.S. Centennial of Flight Commission: The Korean War

U.S. Centennial of Flight Commission

Air Power: The Korean War - Microsoft Internet Explorer

File Edit View Favorites Tools Help

Address http://www.centennialofflight.gov/essay/Air_Power/korea/AP38G2.htm

B-29 Superfortress of the Far East Air Forces 19th Bomber Group on its 150th combat mission since the start of the

The U.S. Centennial of Flight Commission Web site provides an overview of the air war in Korea, including descriptions and photographs of both American and Soviet fighter planes.

Access this Web site from http://www.myreportlinks.com

▶ Turning Out the Lights

The new strategy struck at North Korea's industrial targets to undermine morale. On May 12, 1952, while the plans were being drawn up, the leadership of the UNC changed once again. General Mark W. Clark assumed command from General Matthew Ridgway. The new UNC commander supported the new strategy, which was put into use on June 23, 1952, with UNC air strikes hitting several important hydroelectric plants in North Korea.[39] Those plants supplied most of the electricity for the area and a large portion of northern China. Unlike roads or bridges that were bombed, the plants were difficult to repair or replace, and electrical power was soon out in much of North Korea. The UNC kept hitting these plants and other facilities as the North Koreans tried to rebuild them to generate electricity again.

The UNC's focus turned to Pyongyang, the capital of North Korea and a major industrial and railroad center. The city was bombed twice. Mines, factories, and oil refineries were targeted. Although the air campaign alone did not bring the Communists closer to a cease-fire agreement, it did weaken their ability to keep the war going. Mao Zedong and Kim Il Sung tried to get Joseph Stalin to agree to an armistice, but Stalin refused.[40]

Negotiations dragged on in Panmunjom. The details of the cease-fire were worked out by May 1952, but the negotiators continued to disagree about how prisoner exchanges would be handled. The UNC demanded voluntary repatriation, which meant that prisoners of war could choose whether they wanted to be returned to their country or not.[41] The Communists, however, did not want large numbers of prisoners choosing not to return to China or North Korea. That would have been an embarrassment to their Communist ideology of providing their citizens an ideal society.

Life for Prisoners of War

The situation was worsened by the terrible conditions that existed in prisoner-of-war, or POW, camps. UNC prisoners in North Korean camps were mistreated, and many died from starvation and neglect.

Wide Angle: A State of Mind: Time Line of the Korean War

This PBS site provides a chronological history of the Korean War from the perspective of North Korea. Archival photographs are included.

Access this Web site from http://www.myreportlinks.com

When the Chinese CPV entered the war and took control of prison camps, the treatment of prisoners changed for the better, although the Chinese used political indoctrination, or brainwashing, trying to win the UNC prisoners over to their Communist ideology and beliefs. They also separated the officers from the enlisted men, putting them in different camps.[42] Often, the Chinese guards taunted prisoners by saying that rather than imprisoning them, they were saving them from the Korean people. Considering the abusive treatment of UNC prisoners at the hands of the North Koreans, there was more than a little truth to their statements.[43]

North Korean and Chinese soldiers captured by the UNC faced no such political indoctrination. Many were kept in conditions not much worse than they had endured at home, and some were better fed than they had been before being taken prisoner. However, Communist prisoners faced a similar indifference from their captors. While the UNC captors did make sure that their prisoners were given adequate food and medical care, they basically left them in their compounds on their own. That proved to be a grave mistake when the prisoners themselves began running the camps. The Chinese even trained men to be captured by the UNC forces so that they could organize prison revolts in the Pusan prison camps and on Koje-do Island. The CPV and North Koreans wanted these operatives to stage a major uprising to draw attention to the conditions in the UNC camps and score a propaganda victory for the Communists.

▷ Camp Uprisings

The operatives were surprisingly effective.[44] In the summer of 1951, prisoner unrest and rebellious incidents occurred in Koje-do. There were demonstrations and incidents of prisoners killing other prisoners as well as an organized attack on UNC captors. On May 7, 1952, Koje-do prisoners seized the prison's commandant, General Francis T. Dodd. After several days of negotiations, Dodd was released unharmed, but the incident was an embarrassment for the UNC.[45] Prison riots and uprisings continued for the rest of the war.

Eisenhower Succeeds Truman

On November 4, 1952, Dwight D. Eisenhower, the general who had engineered the Allied victory in Europe during World War II, was elected president of the United States. Eisenhower had pledged during his campaign to bring an end to the fighting in Korea. Many thought he would return to the strategy of a decisive total victory. Just before the elections, General Clark, the UNC commander, suspended cease-fire talks and asked to escalate the conflict to

Generals Mark Clark, left, and James Van Fleet, right, escort President-elect Dwight D. Eisenhower, center, on his visit to American forces in Korea on December 7, 1952. Eisenhower had pledged during his campaign to end the war in Korea.

break the stalemate. Clark's plan was to force the CPV and North Koreans to accept an armistice on UNC terms. The plan also included the use of atomic weapons if that did not work.

By the beginning of 1953, China and North Korea were both suffering economically. Communist China had a tremendous national debt because the Chinese government had to purchase all of the war material it received from the Soviet Union. At home, the Chinese people were sick of war, having endured World War II, a civil war, and now the war in Korea.

North Korea, whose economy had not been strong before the war, had been reduced to little more than rubble. Soviet premier Joseph Stalin, however, wanted to continue the war so that it would be a constant drain on western, and in particular, American, military resources and morale. He believed that a settlement or defeat in Korea would damage Communist prestige worldwide. With Stalin's death, on March 5, 1953, the last major obstacle to a cease-fire was removed.[46]

The Negotiations Continue

By May 1953, both sides were back negotiating and had reached an agreement in principle about prisoners of war. Not all the details had been worked out, however, and the talks broke down once again. The lagging negotiations made the CPV think that the UNC would never negotiate a settlement. The Communists had also made more concessions at the negotiating table, so CPV commanders decided to attempt to save their reputations by keeping up the pressure on the battlefield. The CPV launched an attack on a bulge in the UNC lines called the Kumsong Bulge. The South Korean forces were pushed back for two or three miles but managed to slow the CPV advance and finally stop it, even though fighting continued.[47]

Each side still believed that the other would need to be forced to come to a final agreement in the peace negotiations. The UNC stepped up its bombing attacks, hitting dams in North Korea to flood the country's vital rice fields and starve its people. It had not attacked these targets before because such a strategy would escalate the conflict and cause great suffering on the civilian population.

Not convinced that even those tactics would be enough, the UNC planned a more decisive assault on North Korea that included the possible use of atomic weapons. The Eisenhower administration leaked some of this information through diplomatic channels, indicating that if the next round of peace talks failed, the UNC would escalate the conflict. The UNC presented its final peace settlement for an armistice to take effect on July 27, 1953. On June 16, the Communists finally agreed to a cease-fire.[48]

▶ An Uneasy Peace

While the UNC and the Chinese and North Koreans agreed on the terms of the armistice, the South Korean government did not. Many South Koreans

Even as peace talks continued, American troops and other UNC forces continued to be wounded and killed in Korea. This injured U.S. Marine waits for transportation to a field hospital.

protested because the armistice neither unified Korea under the Republic of Korea nor called for the removal of Chinese forces from the Korean peninsula. Syngman Rhee, the president of South Korea, released 25,000 North Korean prisoners of war in violation of the terms of the agreement, which infuriated the Communists because those prisoners could choose to remain in South Korea.[49] The South Korean government conceded only when the United States promised to sign a security treaty with the Republic of Korea.

▶ The Armistice

To punish the South Korean government for its actions, the Communists ordered one final assault on the South Korean Army. The attack did not succeed, and the CPV forces were pushed back another five miles. After this final assault, the Chinese, the North Koreans, and the United Nations signed an armistice on July 27, 1953, and the fighting in the Korean War finally came to a close.[50]

The preamble to the armistice stated the reasons that the leaders involved had finally reached an agreement to stop the fighting on the Korean peninsula.

The undersigned, the Commander-in-Chief, United Nations Command, on the one hand, and the Supreme Commander of the Korean People's Army and the Commander of the Chinese People's Volunteers, on the other hand, in the interest of stopping the Korean

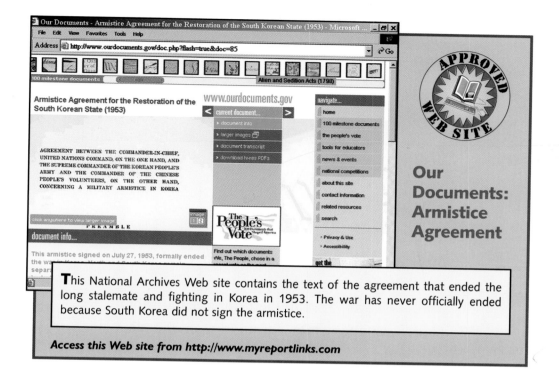

Our Documents - Armistice Agreement for the Restoration of the South Korean State (1953) - Microsoft ...

Address http://www.ourdocuments.gov/doc.php?flash=true&doc=85

100 milestone documents

Alien and Sedition Acts (1798)

Armistice Agreement for the Restoration of the South Korean State (1953)

www.ourdocuments.gov

< current document... >

> document info
> larger images
> document transcript
> download hi-res PDFs

navigate...

home
100 milestone documents
the people's vote
tools for educators
news & events
national competitions
about this site
contact information
related resources
search

> Privacy & Use
> Accessibility

AGREEMENT BETWEEN THE COMMANDER-IN-CHIEF, UNITED NATIONS COMMAND, ON THE ONE HAND, AND THE SUPREME COMMANDER OF THE KOREAN PEOPLE'S ARMY AND THE COMMANDER OF THE CHINESE PEOPLE'S VOLUNTEERS, ON THE OTHER HAND, CONCERNING A MILITARY ARMISTICE IN KOREA

click anywhere to view larger image

PREAMBLE

image 18

The People's Vote

document info...

This armistice signed on July 27, 1953, formally ended the war...

Find out which documents We, The People, chose in a

get the

Our Documents: Armistice Agreement

This National Archives Web site contains the text of the agreement that ended the long stalemate and fighting in Korea in 1953. The war has never officially ended because South Korea did not sign the armistice.

Access this Web site from http://www.myreportlinks.com

conflict, with its great toll of suffering and bloodshed on both sides, and with the objective of establishing an armistice which will insure a complete cessation of hostilities and of all acts of armed force in Korea until a final peaceful settlement is achieved, do individually, collectively, and mutually agree to accept and to be bound and governed by the conditions and terms of armistice set forth in the following Articles and Paragraphs, which said conditions and terms are intended to be purely military in character and to pertain solely to the belligerents in Korea.[51]

The war that had never been declared ended without accomplishing peace between North Korea and South Korea. More than fifty years later, the Korean peninsula remains divided at the 38th parallel, and any hope of a unified Korea remains elusive.

LIFE ON THE FRONT

Soldiers' accounts of life on the front lines during the Korean War provide a vivid picture of how difficult the conditions were. Their accounts also, however, reveal their remarkable ability to appreciate life while constantly on the alert for enemy fire.

James Brady, a U.S. Marine and Virginia native, recalls what life was like for him in Korea when he was not under enemy fire:

When you weren't fighting, the war was pretty good. Mornings were the best time, the terror of night ended, . . . When there was snow in the night, it lay smooth and untracked, no industrial smokestack or city's soot turning it dour and gray, no vehicles to churn it into slush. It hung, glistening, on the pine branches until the sun, warming as it rose, thawed it into tiny, shining icicles. . . . Men crawled out of the bunkers into the morning calm, the industrious using entrenching tools to dig away the snow, tidying the trench. One imaginative fellow after each snow crafted a small snowman on the reserve slope a few yards from his bunker. Eventually there was a formation of them, . . . some hunched gnomelike by earlier thaws, each with a cigar butt rakishly affixed

http://www.dwightdeisenhower.com/koreanwar/Santa delivering presents.jpg - Microsoft Internet Explorer

File   Edit   View   Favorites   Tools   Help

Address   http://www.dwightdeisenhower.com/koreanwar/Santa%20delivering%20presents.jpg   Go

Lighthearted moments do exist in the midst of war. An American soldier in Korea dons a Santa costume to hand out gifts to Korean children. This image and others are found on the **Dwight D. Eisenhower Presidential Library: Primary Sources—The Korean War** Web page.

EDITOR'S CHOICE

in the center of a gargoyle's face. . . . You had lived through another night, you were healthy. . . .

Times like that were rare and wonderful, and even the stench became familiar and nearly welcomed.[1]

Brady also recalls the relaxed quiet times at breakfast between fighting.

Mornings were coffee or cocoa, as hot as you could stand it, the ration cans of fruit, the syrup heavy and sugared. Unless there was serious shelling or heavy snow, after breakfast I walked the half mile along the ridgeline to the company command post. . . . Then we sat around gossiping, the way men do. By now it was maybe ten in the morning, and if the wind wasn't too bad we sat outside on the lip of the trench, smoking and talking, men easy with one another and relaxed.[2]

Life in a Foxhole

Australian Maurie Pears recalls life in the trenches. Pears was part of the Australian contingent of the Commonwealth Division, which fought alongside United States troops in Korea as part of the UNC forces. Pears describes the inconveniences of living in foxholes and bunkers along the line, an inconvenience shared by all UNC troops.

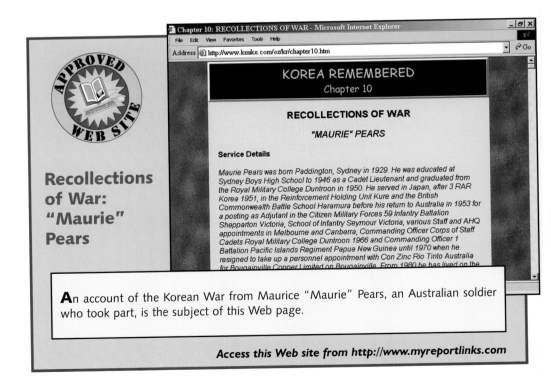

Recollections of War: "Maurie" Pears

APPROVED WEB SITE

Chapter 10: RECOLLECTIONS OF WAR - Microsoft Internet Explorer

File Edit View Favorites Tools Help

Address http://www.kmike.com/oz/kr/chapter10.htm   Go

KOREA REMEMBERED
Chapter 10

RECOLLECTIONS OF WAR

"MAURIE" PEARS

Service Details

Maurie Pears was born Paddington, Sydney in 1929. He was educated at Sydney Boys High School to 1946 as a Cadet Lieutenant and graduated from the Royal Military College Duntroon in 1950. He served in Japan, after 3 RAR Korea 1951, in the Reinforcement Holding Unit Kure and the British Commonwealth Battle School Haramura before his return to Australia in 1953 for a posting as Adjutant in the Citizen Military Forces 59 Infantry Battalion Shepparton Victoria, School of Infantry Seymour Victoria, various Staff and AHQ appointments in Melbourne and Canberra, Commanding Officer Corps of Staff Cadets Royal Military College Duntroon 1966 and Commanding Officer 1 Battalion Pacific Islands Regiment Papua New Guinea until 1970 when he resigned to take up a personnel appointment with Con Zinc Rio Tinto Australia for Bougainville Copper Limited on Bougainville. From 1980 he has lived on the

An account of the Korean War from Maurice "Maurie" Pears, an Australian soldier who took part, is the subject of this Web page.

Access this Web site from http://www.myreportlinks.com

Holes in the ground don't make healthy homes! In the summer we were pestered with flies, mites, rashes and diarrhoea. . . . Winter was just as tough. Frostbite and metal burn, especially on patrol at night, was fearsome. The cold at times would freeze a cup of coffee in the open and you had to shave in the bottom of the hutchie [bunker] to prevent the water freezing on your face. . . . Every time we came back into the line into new positions we faced dirty hutchies and weapon pits left over from the previous occupants. It took days to clean them up and bring them to our Battalion standard. Our first task was always a spring clean. . . . For all this the Digger [Australian equivalent of American GI] received the basic soldier's wage, a bottle of beer in reserve for which he paid and a thankless return home.[3]

Words From Home and From the Front

Mail call is always an important time for soldiers in a war zone—any words of life back home can be a great comfort. Paul Steppe, a Marine from Morgantown, North Carolina, remembers how anxiously he and others waited for news and packages from home to arrive, where something as simple as Spam, a chopped loaf of mostly pork in a can, was treasured.

Mail and packages from home were very important to everyone, especially packages, and in particular, large, nice ones regardless of their condition when received, squashed or otherwise. The receiver of the package

In November 1951, Private First Class Dwight Exe, 5th Cavalry Regiment, found a quiet spot during a break in the fighting to write a letter home. Soldiers' letters from Korea reached their loved ones about a week after they were sent.

becomes the most popular fellow in the squad, and as you open your package, you notice that there are people waiting in line that you have never seen before. Where did they come from? Everyone waiting for handouts! The vagabonds took anything you gave them, but if what they saw didn't appeal to them, they fled like flies and the line dispersed as quickly as it formed. Canned spam was one of our favorite items to receive and to disperse to our bunker buddies. Two cans could feed six buddies for a good evening meal and breakfast. Everyone in our squad shared what they received, even if it was just a single cookie.[4]

American soldiers in Korea were not supposed to keep diaries, because if the soldiers were killed or captured, their writings could provide intelligence to the enemy. Marine James Brady was able to scribble a few notes, however, and acted as his own censor in the letters he wrote home so that his family would not worry about him.

I kept a few notes in the little spiral notebook in my breast pocket, writing very small to conserve pages, and in pencil. If you got wet, and we were always getting wet, ink ran. And I composed my letters home very carefully, describing as accurately as I could the land and the weather and the sense of place, on the cheap airmail flimsy they parceled out to us and which we could send without a stamp. . . . And so I wrote about Korea and the men, self-censoring things that might frighten my family or friends, and sent off little essays and brief reports of war, knowing one day I might see those letters again and remember.[5]

Brady was able to write letters that would not upset his loved ones because he was capable of appreciating those moments not spent in combat.

If you have never been to war you cannot realize that some of it—not all, of course—is such sheer, boyish fun. You lived outdoors, you were physically active, you shared the boisterous camaraderie of other young men, you shed fat and put on sinew and muscle. . . .

You saw the dawn and the night stars and came to calculate time and date by the phases of the moon, and on those rare days of thaw you heard the gurgle of running water under the snow, heading toward the valleys and the sea. You smelled the pines and listened to the wind and could sense when snow was coming and knew to the instant when the sun would rise, when the sun would set.[6]

▶ A Place of Extremes

Not all soldiers felt as Brady did when it came to the weather conditions in the Korean peninsula. With rugged, mountainous territory, Korea was a place of hot summers and freezing cold winters— some of the coldest conditions ever faced by American forces in a major combat zone. Marine Lieutenant Joseph Owen, a World War II veteran, was involved in the combat around the Chosin Reservoir as the Marines tried to fight their way out of a CPV trap. Owen recalls the cold being as dangerous as the Chinese he was facing.

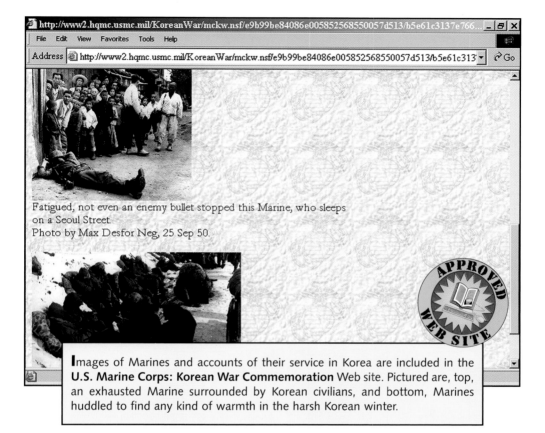

http://www2.hqmc.usmc.mil/KoreanWar/mckw.nsf/e9b99be84086e005852568550057d513/b5e61c3137e766... _ 🗗 ✕

File   Edit   View   Favorites   Tools   Help

Address 🔎 http://www2.hqmc.usmc.mil/KoreanWar/mckw.nsf/e9b99be84086e005852568550057d513/b5e61c313 ▼   ↻ Go

Fatigued, not even an enemy bullet stopped this Marine, who sleeps on a Seoul Street.
Photo by Max Desfor Neg, 25 Sep 50.

APPROVED WEB SITE

Images of Marines and accounts of their service in Korea are included in the **U.S. Marine Corps: Korean War Commemoration** Web site. Pictured are, top, an exhausted Marine surrounded by Korean civilians, and bottom, Marines huddled to find any kind of warmth in the harsh Korean winter.

The cold weather was as formidable an enemy as the Chinese. The troops, never prone to minimize a problem, declared that temperature readings were down to thirty below, Fahrenheit. There was a thermometer back at regiment, and the daily action reports confirmed the troops' judgment. Rarely did the reports exceed zero degrees, and there were lows of twenty below.

When we weren't on the move, we were freezing cold and we spent much of our energy trying to get warm. Battalion had warming stations—big pyramid tents with kerosene stoves in them—which we rarely used because they were far from our company

Trying to locate enemy positions, American soldiers with the 19th Infantry Regiment make their way over snow-covered mountains north of Seoul in January 1951.

▲ Soldiers in Korea suffered the most brutal winter weather to hit the peninsula in a century. Here, frostbitten troops from the 1st Marine Division and 7th Infantry Division who survived the battle at the Chosin Reservoir, "the Frozen Chosin," wait for planes to pick them up.

perimeters. Up on the line we had only our own body warmth, which we tried to keep enclosed within the parkas. At night, in the fox holes, the men pressed together to preserve whatever warmth they could generate.

We wore woolen caps under the helmets that kept our ears from freezing. The hoods of the parkas went over the helmets and provided some protection from the bitter winds, but they obscured our peripheral vision. We seldom removed the knitted gloves that we wore under the canvas mittens. Bare fingers, we found, froze to metal; they froze to weapons, bayonets, buckles—whatever we touched.[7]

Paul Steppe also remembers how brutally cold it was on the MLR, the front line of contact between the UNC troops and Communist forces, where good boots were worth more than gold.

The best part of my equipment, aside from my weapons, were the new boots issued in late fall. Everyone had seen movies about the seriousness of taking care of their feet. The gravity of that was due to the many foot soldiers of the various countries fighting under the United Nations Colors getting frozen feet during the winter of 1950. Many toes, feet, and legs were amputated due to frostbite that was either not treated immediately due to the war situation or ignored by the afflicted. These newly issued boots that I now have were a gift from Heaven. Requiring only one pair of socks, the boots are water-proof and insulated and have at least an inch and a half sole and larger heel. They are a little heavy but absolutely great! They keep my feet warm and comfortable.[8]

▶ A Chaplain's Concern for Koreans

Even in the midst of fighting, brutal weather, and the fight to stay alive, some soldiers were also concerned for the people of Korea who were made refugees by the war. Frank Griepp, a chaplain for the 7th Cavalry, wrote the following letter to his wife on December 2, 1950, after an all-night march. In it, he wished his wife a happy birthday, and although he missed her, he told her that he would not have wanted her to see the suffering he was seeing in Korea.

My heart bleeds for these people, the civilians. I guess they have been turned out of their homes so often they know what to take in a hurry. The Chinese Commie sldrs [soldiers] mix in with them, so we can't take any chances. Just have to move all natives out of an area we occupy, not only so we can use their homes, but to avoid danger of infiltration. So we see them on the

▲ Even in the midst of war—or perhaps because of it—soldiers in the U.S. Army's 31st Regiment took time to attend a service led by Army chaplain Kenny Lynch, August 28, 1951, north of Hwachon.

A letter from an Army chaplain to his wife mentioned his concern for the people of Korea who were suffering as a result of the war. His letters and others are found on the **Wisconsin War Letters: The Korean War** Web site of the University of Wisconsin.

EDITOR'S CHOICE

roads, hurrying along, babies & little children tied on their backs, a bedroll on a little food & clothing on their heads. Poorly clothed, bare legged often, tiny babies often bareheaded. Sometimes a group will have a little pony or cow used as a pack animal. . . . Where they go for shelter at nite, I don't know.[9]

UNDER FIRE AND IMPRISONED

Living in alien surroundings in uncomfortable conditions is difficult enough. Being a soldier in a war means facing the dangers of enemy fire and constant risk of terrible injuries or death.

Marine Lieutenant Joseph Owen recalled a squad action around Chosin Reservoir in November 1950 led by Lieutenant Chew Een Lee, an Asian-American Marine. The son of Chinese immigrants, Lee put his men through rigorous drills to get them ready for combat. Most fighting in Korea was done at the squad level, which involved small, quick, and often brutal fights between small groups of men.

It was an article of faith with Chew Een Lee that combat leadership came from the front. In the attack, he positioned himself with the most advanced squad, just behind the point. He wore a bright, fluorescent-pink vest fashioned of cloth panels that he had obtained from the tactical air team. The intended purpose of the brilliantly colored panels was to mark the forward extent of our lines for supporting aircraft. Lee wore his vest so that his men could locate him quickly during a firefight.

He still had a sling on his wounded right arm, and he carried his carbine [rifle] in his left hand. He fired

▲ *Marines use ladders to go ashore at Inchon on September 15, 1950. The invasion at Inchon marked an end to a string of North Korean victories and allowed the UNC forces to recapture Seoul.*

it from the hip, using it to shoot tracers that marked target sectors. [Tracers are bullets treated with chemicals so that they will leave a trail of light momentarily.]

A few days after we began patrolling the country above Koto-ri, I took a tracer bullet mortar squad out with Lee's platoon. That day the Chinese departed from form and gave us a stiff fight. Halfway up a hill that was sparsely covered with shrub, they opened up on Lee. He was with the point fire team and, wearing his glowing pink vest, was very visible to the enemy as

An infantryman wounded in combat waits to be evacuated to an aid station behind the front lines in February 1951.

well as his own men. I expected to see him get hit, an easy target, but he did not go down. . . .[1]

Despite heavy attacks and injury, Lee reorganized his platoon and moved his men up the slope held by the enemy. He surveyed the area so that his machine gun posts could be set up in a better defensive position. Owen recalls Lee's strategy and heroism.

The Chinese found it difficult to defend against Lee's energetic tactics. Our coordinated mortar and machine gun fire kept them pinned to the ground. . . .

The Chinese withdrew. . . . When he was certain that the Chinese would not counterattack, Lee ordered us all off the hill. . . . On the return march to the company perimeter, no one complained about Lieutenant Lee's excessive training methods. He walked along the column and thanked the men for their good work. I wondered to myself how many firefights Lee would survive, standing at the front of his troops clad in that brilliant pink vest.[2]

▶ First Kill

Marine Paul Steppe describes his first time under fire and the first time he killed an enemy soldier, one of the North Korean People's Army (NKPA).

With every mortar shell that came in screaming, I thought it had my name on it. My eyes caught something moving to my left about thirty yards away. I turned and saw an NKPA soldier moving southward on another smaller ridge line consisting of soft dirt or sand, which made running away difficult. I sighted him with my rifle and pulled the trigger. I know that I hit him, but so did about four other marines. The guy was picked up off the ground from the impact of the bullets and moved sideways about a yard and fell dead. I didn't feel any remorse for that soldier, perhaps because I was not the only one that shot him. I had heard that the first kill was the most difficult, and many marines were killed because they hesitated in squeezing the trigger before the enemy did. The soldier was running away from battle. He could have been shot by his own colleagues.

That was the way it was, waiting, attacking, digging holes, attacking, waiting, and more hills to climb up and down. That was Korea and its famous mountain ranges. Engagements were sometimes swift with little defensive reaction, but often they became fierce, and men were killed or injured and most were never seen again.[3]

When Steppe saw his own friends being killed, he began to see war as senseless.

I think your worst war memories are your buddies being killed. It's a buddy system. You have a bond and brotherhood when you're overseas. Watch the man on the left, you watch the man on the right, and they do the same for you. They do best by replacing that man as soon as possible, to keep you talking, to keep you occupied. I lost six buddies over there. And they were senseless. That's when I started considering war senseless, when I started losing my buddies.[4]

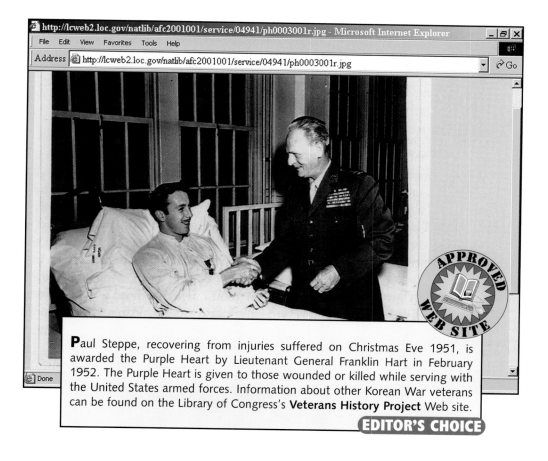

Paul Steppe, recovering from injuries suffered on Christmas Eve 1951, is awarded the Purple Heart by Lieutenant General Franklin Hart in February 1952. The Purple Heart is given to those wounded or killed while serving with the United States armed forces. Information about other Korean War veterans can be found on the Library of Congress's **Veterans History Project** Web site.

EDITOR'S CHOICE

Enemy attacks came suddenly and unexpectedly. Paul Steppe had sentry duty on December 24, 1951, when a grenade "found him."

While scanning areas toward my left, I heard a "pop" over my head to the right flank. I knew it was a grenade because I saw the fuse from the Russian grenade flicker several times. I yelled out, "Fire in the hole," and bent forward and heard another "pop." By then I was bent over on my knees and partially around a corner of the trench. Both grenades landed to my rear and exploded. The first one merely threw dirt all over the place, but the second one found me. It blew

my right boot completely off with its shrapnel and
injured my right foot and buttocks.[5]

The weather made the fighting even worse.
Lieutenant Joseph Owen recalls the tricks that
soldiers and medics relied on to keep themselves
alive and their equipment working under hostile
conditions.

Weapons froze and seized up when we used lubricating
oil on them. They slowed or jammed when we didn't.
The machine guns and BARs [Browning Automatic
Rifles] were most affected; on first firing they would

Address http://korea50.army.mil/images/army/soldier_comforting.shtml

A grief stricken American infantryman whose buddy has been

The aftermath of battle: An American infantryman grieves for a friend killed in
action. This image and others are featured on **United States of America:
Korean War Commemoration,** a Web site of the U.S. Department of Defense.

hesitate two or three seconds between rounds, then slowly build up to their regular rate of fire. Hair tonic, with alcohol in it, became a fairly effective substitute lubricant.

The cold forced the corpsmen to change their way of doing business. With the first sounds of a firefight they would take several syrettes of morphine and put them in their mouths. This kept the morphine liquid until the syrettes were jabbed into a wounded man's flesh to relieve his pain.

The corpsmen were the only ones who worked with bare hands in the severe cold, and they found a way to keep their fingers nimble while tending a wounded man. The heat of the man's blood did the trick, or his guts, as they were stuffed back into the belly.[6]

Twenty-year-old private Ted Brush was in Korea for only two months before he sustained multiple wounds in combat. He described his ordeal in a letter to his parents in Richfield, Idaho:

Dear Folks,

I supposed you have already received a telegram saying that I was wounded in action. I am now in a hospital at Tajon, South Korea, about 30 miles behind the front line. I was hit by two grenades. We went into the assault up a hill and the Chinks [an uncomplimentary term for Chinese] just stayed in their holes and threw out grenades. I dodged around still keeping moving forward but slowing down cause grenades were all over. . . . I knelt down to put a new magazine [bullet or cartridge holder] in my B.A.R. when a rocket shrapnel from a grenade behind me hit me right along the left jaw. I saw blood spurting and my face went numb so I called to my foxhole buddy (Kelly) to take my B.A.R.

I was just handing it to him when someone yelled "Grenade!" I started to hit the dirt and Kelly kind of fell away when I felt myself get hit in the right leg. A curious feeling went up my leg and then I got hit in the right cheek. I fell down and felt blood running in my boot and looked at Kelly, he was holding his hand and motioned for me to come back where he was but I couldn't make it. I just laid there praying, half afraid I was going to bleed to death. I was calling a medic but I couldn't see one. About ½ hour later, one showed up and bandaged me, another guy had tried to move me, but I couldn't hardly move. I laid there for about another hour and ½, hollering for a litter. (I could hear my squad leader cussing and yelling to get one for me too, when I noticed bullets kicking up dust and found out a sniper was firing at me, so I crawled over the hill.)

They're about ready to put me on the train to Pusan so [I] will close. I have a broken leg so maybe I'll get home. I am fine, but it still hurts a little. Will write tomorrow so don't worry. The medical corps is doing a good job on me.

Love,

Ted

P.S. We lost a lot of men on that hill. The # of the hill is 477.[7]

▶ Life as a POW

Many of the Americans and other UNC forces captured by the North Koreans and Chinese during the war were treated brutally, although the Chinese generally treated their prisoners better than the Koreans did. Even so, many American POWs died

Wounded 1st Cavalry Division soldiers at an aid station outside Yongdong, July 25, 1950. Follow - Micros...

File   Edit   View   Favorites   Tools   Help

Address http://www.trumanlibrary.org/korea/photos/35percentdmg7_24.htm   Go

Done

Wounded soldiers receive care at an aid station near Yongdong, Korea, July 1950. This photograph and other archival materials of the Korean War come from **Korea+50: No Longer Forgotten,** a Web site from the presidential libraries of Harry S Truman and Dwight D. Eisenhower.

EDITOR'S CHOICE

during captivity. For some of those who survived, the experience remained too painful to talk about for years afterward.

Harley Coon dropped out of high school in 1948 to join the Army. He served in Japan with B Company of the 35th Regiment, 25th Infantry Division, stationed at Camp Otsu, where he witnessed Japanese prisoners of war returning from captivity in Russia. He described his work with them: "The majority of the Japanese that I dealt with had been working in Siberian salt mines.

We had to literally drag them out, give them baths and clothes. They were then given tickets and Yen [money] and told to go home. Most of them were scared to death or in shock, I'm not sure which."[8]

When the Korean War began, Coon and others were sent to Pusan. He and five members of his company were captured in North Korea by the Chinese on November 27, 1950. Coon described his capture: "We were put into a circle and surrounded by machine guns with full bandoleers [belts that feed ammunition to a machine gun]. We had heard that this was the way that other prisoners had been slaughtered."[9]

They were not killed, but they were forced to march from one camp to another. Coon described the conditions:

The first camp we ended up in we called "Bean Camp" because we ate soybean paste rolled up into the shape of apples. From there, I was sent to "Death Valley" for about eight to 10 days. There were so many men dying that we covered their bodies with anything that we could find. We started marching again. We'd march for a few days, stop, then march again. We ended up in Camp 5 in Puck'tong, sometime in January.[10]

Camp 5 held between four thousand and five thousand prisoners, divided by rank, race, and level of education. Coon's wit and imagination helped him to endure the interrogation by his captors and the terrible conditions of imprisonment in Camp 5:

▲ *No longer prisoners of war, these American servicemen face reporters after being released in September 1953. Their release was part of Operation Big Switch, the final exchange of POWs in Korea that lasted until December 23, 1953.*

We were housed in space that forced us to sleep toe to head. One morning I woke up and it looked like it had snowed; both men on either side of me had died. There were pathways where we carried stretchers of the 50–60 men who died daily. Usually four or five of us were on a burial detail. The same guy that was on the detail often was the same guy that we buried that evening. In Camp 5, there were about 1,600–2,000 men buried. I wondered why I was being spared.[11]

Harley Coon was finally released to American forces on August 31, 1953, after thirty-three months and four days as a prisoner of war. He did not speak of that imprisonment with other ex-POWs of the Korean War until 1975, when he got in touch with a buddy he had served with. Coon became more involved with the Korean War ex-POW movement in 1988, after attending a lecture on Americans in war. Not one mention was made of Korea, and when Coon asked the speaker why, he was told that his service in Korea had only been a "police action."[12]

Sergeant Major Cleveland, above, weapons squad leader of the 2nd Infantry Division, directs his machine gun crew to the position of the North Korean forces north of the Chongchon River in November 1950.

▶ Under Fire From Two Fronts

For African Americans serving in the Korean War, enemy soldiers were not the only problem. In the beginning of the war, black soldiers were still segregated from white soldiers, even though President Harry Truman had ordered the armed forces to integrate in 1948. With the high casualty rate suffered by American soldiers in Korea, however, combat units quickly became short-handed.

American military leaders began to send large numbers of black troops to fight alongside white troops.

The Chinese tried to exploit the racial tensions of the time by dropping leaflets intended for African-American soldiers. The leaflets, while propaganda, asked a question that some of those soldiers were already asking themselves: Why were they fighting in a war thousands of miles away when they were not treated as equal citizens back home in the United States? Curtis Morrow, who saw combat in Korea, recalled his reaction:

> We all saw those pictures of a black man being hung and a bunch of white faces eating popcorn and little kids jeering and laughing and in the caption beneath the picture they would have "Why are you here? Why are you fighting us? Is this what you're fighting for?"[13]

Samuel King, another African-American veteran of the Korean War, remembered how the propaganda made him feel.

> It was an embarrassment for us to have someone in a foreign country know how we were being treated. And we over here fighting these people to make it better for someone back home and we get back home and it's not going to be any better and we knew that, yet and still we had a job to do and we felt that we should do it.[14]

Despite the injustice that still existed at home, integrated military units learned how to work together in Korea because their lives depended on it. John Cannon, an African-American paratrooper who served in Korea, spoke of the color blindness of combat that forged bonds between soldiers of different races:

You've heard that there's no atheists in foxholes? There are no bigots. You want somebody! They could be polka dot and you get to love him. You get to love him. He gets to look out for you. You get to look out for him and all of that . . . dies. It just dies.[15]

THE POLITICS OF WAR AND THE AMERICAN PUBLIC

Twentieth-century wars were fought in the field but directed by governments located miles from the front. Those governments sometimes failed to match their ideas about conducting war to what was actually happening on the battlefield, which affected military decisions there.

President Harry S Truman defended the decision to send United States troops to stop the North Korean invasion by saying it would stop the spread of Communism.

In my generation, this was not the first occasion when the strong had attacked the weak. I recalled some earlier instances: Manchuria, Ethiopia, Austria. I remembered how each time that the democracies failed to act it had encouraged the aggressors to keep going ahead. Communism was acting in Korea just as Hitler, Mussolini, and the Japanese had acted ten, fifteen and twenty years earlier. I felt certain that if South Korea was allowed to fall, Communist leaders would be emboldened to override nations close to our own shores. If the Communists were permitted to force their way into the Republic of Korea without opposition from the free world, no small nation would have the courage to resist threats and aggression by stronger Communist neighbors. If this was allowed to

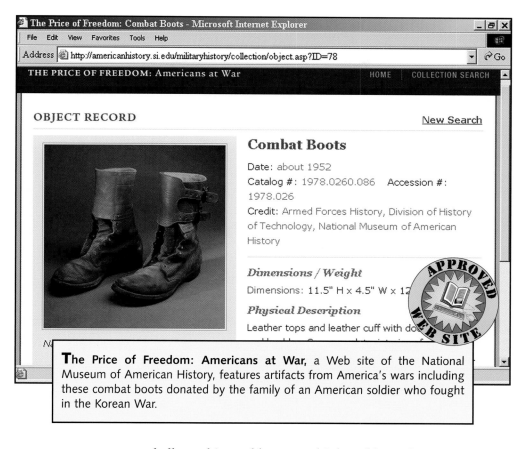

The Price of Freedom: Combat Boots - Microsoft Internet Explorer _ 🗗 ✕

File   Edit   View   Favorites   Tools   Help

Address 🔲 http://americanhistory.si.edu/militaryhistory/collection/object.asp?ID=78   ▼   𝒫 Go

THE PRICE OF FREEDOM: Americans at War   HOME   COLLECTION SEARCH ▲

OBJECT RECORD   New Search

Combat Boots

Date: about 1952

Catalog #: 1978.0260.086   Accession #: 1978.026

Credit: Armed Forces History, Division of History of Technology, National Museum of American History

Dimensions / Weight

Dimensions: 11.5" H x 4.5" W x 1...

Physical Description

Leather tops and leather cuff with do...

The Price of Freedom: Americans at War, a Web site of the National Museum of American History, features artifacts from America's wars including these combat boots donated by the family of an American soldier who fought in the Korean War.

go unchallenged it would mean a third world war, just as similar incidents had brought on the Second World War. It was also clear to me that the foundations and the principles of the United Nations were at stake unless this unprovoked attack on Korea could be stopped.[1]

A presidential order signed two years before the Korean War began would have a great impact on the fighting in Korea. On July 26, 1948, President Truman signed Executive Order 9981, which read as follows: "It is hereby declared to be the policy of the President that there shall be equality of treatment and opportunity for all persons in the armed services without regard to race, color, religion, or national origin."[2] While some American military commanders in Korea were slow to racially integrate their forces, the Korean War became the first war in which white and black Americans fought together in combat in large numbers.

Korean Views

The North Koreans saw the United States' involvement in the affairs of Korea differently than the UNC did. North Korean foreign minister Pak Hon Yong

http://www.army.mil/cmh-pg/photos/Korea/kor1952/SC403717.jpg - Microsoft Internet Explorer

File   Edit   View   Favorites   Tools   Help

Address http://www.army.mil/cmh-pg/photos/Korea/kor1952/SC403717.jpg   Go

The Korean War was the first war fought by Americans in which combat forces were integrated to a large extent. This photograph and others come from **Online Bookshelves: Korean War,** a Web site of the United States Army Center of Military History.

made this statement to the United Nations on September 28, 1950, protesting its intervention and blaming the civil war in Korea on the United States' support of South Korea.

> American intervention and the civil war started by American imperialists and their running dogs headed by Rhee Syngman have inflicted tremendous calamities and hardships upon the Korean people, for which the U.S. government is solely responsible. [Rhee Syngman is Syngman Rhee, South Korea's president; in many Asian languages, the family name precedes the first name.]
>
> Through its official representatives, the United States government supplied the traitorous bandits of Rhee Syngman with political, military and economic aid, and directed in the building and training of Rhee Syngman's army and in working out the aggressive plan for the invasion of North Korea. Such encouragement and aid spurred the Syngman Rhee clique [group of people] to start a civil war in Korea.[3]

▶ "A Few Bombs on Moscow. . ."

Syngman Rhee was convinced that the ultimate goal of the war should have been the reunification of the Korean peninsula under his government. To that end, he never stopped proposing plans to achieve a total victory and even interrupted UNC negotiations for a settlement. In this letter to the American ambassador to South Korea on January 10, 1951, Rhee makes another request for the United States to escalate the war beyond Korea's borders.

 *South Korean president Syngman Rhee, right, meets with General Douglas MacArthur in June 1950. Rhee's demands often put him at odds with the United Nations Command in Korea.*

We pray to God for your health, for everything depends on you now more than ever. Even now you can save the situation by giving us immediate arms and ammunition for our 250,000 trained youth, and later another 250,000 now undergoing training. With these half million men fully armed, in addition to our present fighting strength to help the valiant United Nations forces, we can turn the tide. If we lose this opportunity the Chinese and northern Communists will destroy all our armed forces and most of the anti-Communist civilian population.

What is still worse is the far-reaching effects of this disaster on you and other great leaders who courageously undertook to check the Communist aggression in Korea. They will all try to lay the blame on you, and the Soviets and their puppets all over the world will triumph and rejoice. The United Nations will never save either themselves or others from another world war, but only make that war more disastrous. To save the situation we must do all we can to defeat and destroy the Chinese invaders according to guerrilla tactics, and authorize General MacArthur to use any weapons that will check Communist aggression anywhere, even the atom bomb. A few bombs on Moscow alone will shake the Communist world.[4]

Syngman Rhee was frequently at odds with the UNC leaders, making it even more difficult for the UNC peace negotiators to make real headway in their truce talks. The situation became so tense that the UNC began to consider the possibility of replacing Rhee.

Stopping the Communist Supply Route

From the beginning, the UNC strategy for winning depended on stopping the Communist forces from getting vital supplies and ammunition to the front. A captured Chinese document from November 1950 confirms both the success of that UNC strategy and the shortcomings in the CPV's organization:

A shortage of transportation and escort personnel makes it impossible to accomplish the mission of supplying the troops. As a result, our soldiers frequently starve. From now on, the organization of our rear service units should be improved.

The troops were hungry. They ate cold food, and some had only a few potatoes in two days. They were unable to maintain the physical strength for combat; the wounded personnel could not be evacuated. . . . The fire power of our entire army was basically inadequate. When we used our guns there were no shells and sometimes the shells were duds.[5]

The Bigger Picture

Intelligence is crucial to any war effort. Military commanders need to know not just the battlefield status of an enemy army but also the political situation of a country at war. A U.S. Department of State

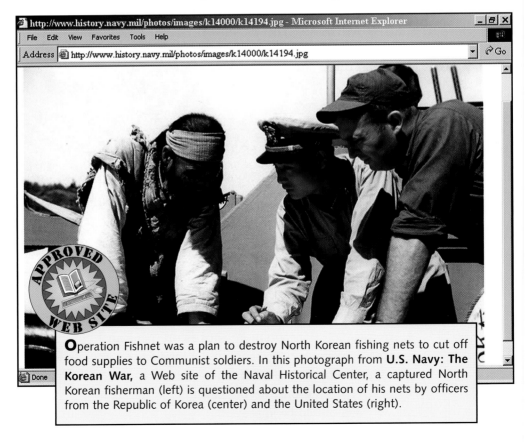

http://www.history.navy.mil/photos/images/k14000/k14194.jpg - Microsoft Internet Explorer

File   Edit   View   Favorites   Tools   Help

Address   http://www.history.navy.mil/photos/images/k14000/k14194.jpg   Go

Done

Operation Fishnet was a plan to destroy North Korean fishing nets to cut off food supplies to Communist soldiers. In this photograph from **U.S. Navy: The Korean War,** a Web site of the Naval Historical Center, a captured North Korean fisherman (left) is questioned about the location of his nets by officers from the Republic of Korea (center) and the United States (right).

research report on North Korea from November 1952 concludes that while North Korean civilian resolve to continue the war was weakening, it was not enough to bring an end to the fighting because the North Korean military machine remained largely intact and loyal:

A major problem facing the north Korean regime has been the serious decline in the morale of the civilian population due to severe and prolonged privation. Recent information indicates that discontent (and possibly even subversion) exists on the home front. The government has repeatedly cautioned the population against reactionary and subversive elements in rear areas who make use of "the restless, discontented, cowardly, [and] revengeful to spy on military secrets, to spread rumors, to alienate the people from the government, and even to assassinate government leaders."

[D]espite weakness in north Korea's own internal security forces, and despite the breakdown of the propaganda machine, popular dissatisfaction and unrest have thus far been contained. This has been due primarily to the fact that Korean police forces have been supplemented and bolstered by small garrisons of Chinese troops stationed in many towns and villages throughout the country. In addition, the North Korean army, which at present mans only a small part of the fighting front, has remained reliable; its morale appears to be considerabl[y] higher than that of the civilian population. Both its reliability and morale have been [e]nsured by continuous indoctrination and surveillance and, further, by sufficient food rations and supplies.[6]

An American soldier holding his eight-month-old son kisses his wife good-bye as he prepares to leave for Korea in 1950. If he was lucky enough to return from war, he most likely did not return to the same kind of homecoming afforded World War II veterans.

The American Public's Reaction to the Korean War

As with all wars, the soldiers and politicians from both sides were not the only ones affected. The Korean War, however, has been called the "Forgotten War" because it is sandwiched between World War II and Vietnam. Many Americans were not certain what to make of the Korean War because it was a limited war—the first time that the American public lived through a conflict that did not end in total victory. The stalemate in Korea was an embarrassment for the United States, which had only eight years earlier managed to bring about the defeat of Germany and Japan in World War II. The American people who had lived through that war wanted peace, and as the Korean War dragged on without any clear victory in sight, American public support for the war waned.

The War and Popular Media

Hollywood, always America's dream factory, seemed to regard Korea as a bad nap—not necessarily a good dream, but not a nightmare either. The movie studios still produced films about World War II that provided a clear victor and a happy ending. Occasionally, they modified films to fit a Korean setting, such as *Fixed Bayonets* and *Combat Squad*. Gregory Peck starred in *Pork Chop Hill*, but that film was more a fight with the government's bureaucracy than with the Communist menace. *The Manchurian Candidate*, on

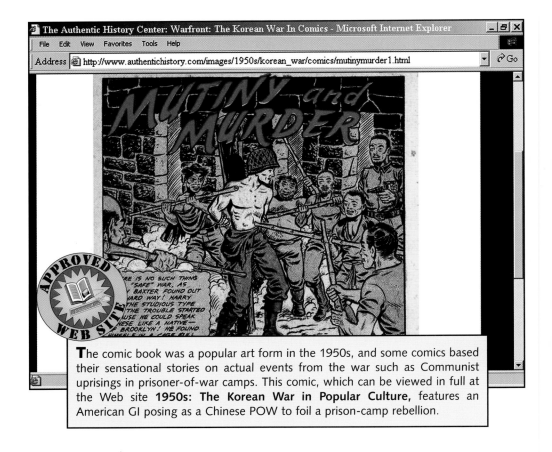

The Authentic History Center: Warfront: The Korean War In Comics - Microsoft Internet Explorer

File   Edit   View   Favorites   Tools   Help

Address   http://www.authentichistory.com/images/1950s/korean_war/comics/mutinymurder1.html   Go

The comic book was a popular art form in the 1950s, and some comics based their sensational stories on actual events from the war such as Communist uprisings in prisoner-of-war camps. This comic, which can be viewed in full at the Web site **1950s: The Korean War in Popular Culture,** features an American GI posing as a Chinese POW to foil a prison-camp rebellion.

the other hand, was a psychological thriller that focused on the rumors of Communist brainwashing of prisoners of war rather than the actual war itself. It also showed Korean War veterans in a poor light, foreshadowing the mixed portrayals of Vietnam veterans by the media less than two decades later. Hollywood seemed to drop the Korean War about the time the Vietnam War provided new, if not better, material.

If film has been unkind to Korea, television has ignored the Korean conflict with one exception. The 1970s television comedy series *M*A*S*H** takes place in a Mobile Army Surgical Hospital unit during the Korean War. The show, based on a critically acclaimed movie from the same era, was extremely popular, although it is widely considered to have been a commentary on the Vietnam War. The series ran eleven years, eight more than the Korean War.

If visual arts barely acknowledged the existence of the Korean War, the music world ignored it completely. Most wars have songs to inspire soldiers and their families back home. The Civil War produced "Battle Hymn of the Republic," "When Johnny Comes Marching Home Again," and "Tenting Tonight." The First World War had "Over There." The Second World War had a variety of songs, including "God Bless America" and "In Der Fuhrer's Face." The Korean War had no such anthem. Composers, like the public, are often inspired by war to write patriotic songs. With the Korean War, however, songwriters, like the American public, seem to have been unsure about a war that the nation's own president referred to as a police action.

COMING HOME

Unlike the parades that greeted American soldiers returning from the two world wars, the homecoming for Korean War veterans reflected the uncertainty of the American people about the war itself. While there had been a clear enemy in the Communist forces, the war's ending without a victory discouraged large public celebrations.

▶ Happiness and Fear

Sometimes, soldiers were sent home in rotations. Private First Class Al Puntasecca, who had served with the artillery, wrote to his family to let them know that he would see them soon. He began by mentioning how much he looked forward to simple things like three meals a day and indoor plumbing.

Dear Everybody,

I'm coming home! It's official as of this morning. It will be some time before I crash in your door, a few weeks, maybe, but, I'm coming home! Remember I told you how seasick I was on the way over here? Well, I can't wait to do it again.

That little house is going to look like a palace to me and, you people like Kings, and, Queens. People who love you. A clean place to live. A clean place to

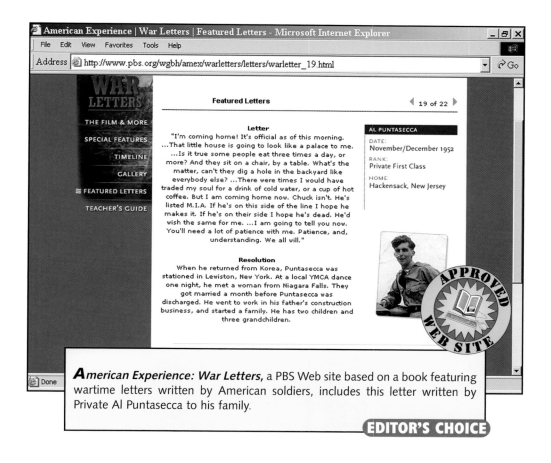

American Experience: War Letters, a PBS Web site based on a book featuring wartime letters written by American soldiers, includes this letter written by Private Al Puntasecca to his family.

EDITOR'S CHOICE

live life. To sleep in a what do you call it, bed? yeah, that's it, bed. Running water. Hot meals. And, what's this I hear about people having private bathrooms, and, private showers? Really? Is it true some people eat three times a day, or, more? and, they sit on a chair, by a table. What's the matter, can't they dig a hole in the back yard like everybody else? . . .[1]

Beyond the humor, Private Puntasecca warned his parents that they might not recognize their son as the same man who left for war.

Yeah. I'm looking forward to seeing you again, but I'm in no hurry to see the expressions on your faces when you see me. I want to see you try to hide the shock on your faces. You might even ask me for proof I'm your son. Don't feel bad. I see it in my own face every day. I have spent 12 months over here. The longest 30 years of my life. A short time ago I was 18, and, all I was worried about was cars, girls, and, how much beer a real man could drink. No more. Don't get me wrong. I still want a hot car, a hot girl, and, a cold beer, but, there were times I could have traded them all for a warm blanket. A wool hat. A pair of gloves, or, ear muffs. another pair of socks. . . . There were times I would have traded my soul for a drink of cold water, or a cup of hot coffee. But, I am coming home now.[2]

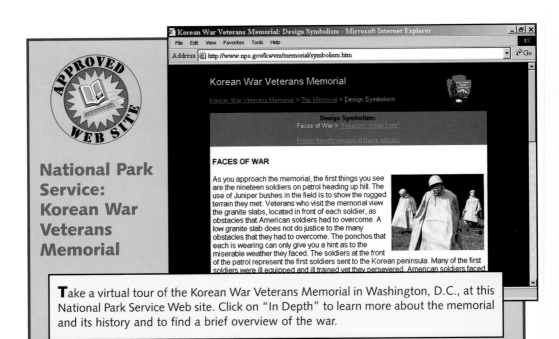

National Park Service: Korean War Veterans Memorial

Korean War Veterans Memorial: Design Symbolism - Microsoft Internet Explorer

File   Edit   View   Favorites   Tools   Help

Address   http://www.nps.gov/kwvm/memorial/symbolism.htm   Go

Korean War Veterans Memorial

Korean War Veterans Memorial > The Memorial > Design Symbolism

Design Symbolism:
Faces of War > "Freedom is Not Free"

Printer friendly version of these articles

FACES OF WAR

As you approach the memorial, the first things you see are the nineteen soldiers on patrol heading up hill. The use of Juniper bushes in the field is to show the rugged terrain they met. Veterans who visit the memorial view the granite slabs, located in front of each soldier, as obstacles that American soldiers had to overcome. A low granite slab does not do justice to the many obstacles that they had to overcome. The ponchos that each is wearing can only give you a hint as to the miserable weather they faced. The soldiers at the front of the patrol represent the first soldiers sent to the Korean peninsula. Many of the first soldiers were ill equipped and ill trained yet they persevered. American soldiers faced

Take a virtual tour of the Korean War Veterans Memorial in Washington, D.C., at this National Park Service Web site. Click on "In Depth" to learn more about the memorial and its history and to find a brief overview of the war.

Access this Web site from http://www.myreportlinks.com

Puntasecca reflected about the absurdity of war that only a soldier who had lived through one could understand.

How many guys have been killed in wars? How many not born because they were killed? Did it start with Cain, and Abel? The caveman? Who? Does it matter? And, for <u>what</u>? What? Has anything changed? Will anything change? No, Never. So what do we do? <u>Nothing</u>! If something could have been done I'm sure somebody would have done it. All we can do, all anybody can do is try to understand.[3]

Finally, he reflected that physical injuries were not always the worst kind and asked his family to be patient with him because he was suffering from wounds that were not visible.

You know, it's almost funny, we see a guy in a wheel chair, a guy on crutches, one arm, hooks for hands, and, we break our backs trying to help him. But, what about the wounds you can't see? The phantoms, the nightmares, the ghosts in your head? I am going to tell you now. you'll need a lot of patience with me. Patience, and, understanding. We all will. See you soon. See you soon. See you soon.
    Jr.[4]

No Recognition

Many Americans returning home from Korea were disappointed at the reception they received from

▲ Catherine Neville, an Army nurse and veteran of World War II, the Korean War, and the Vietnam War, believes one of the reasons that Korean War vets were not welcomed home with great ceremony was because the troops came home in small groups rather than in large units.

a public that was unsure how to treat the war's veterans. Catherine Neville, who served as a nurse in World War II, the Korean War, and the Vietnam War, wrote about some of the reasons why Korean War veterans were not welcomed home with fanfare.

> There were no parades. Well you see you came out as an individual, and I think that's what happened to the Korean veterans as well as the Vietnam veterans. They came home to nothing, but it was because they weren't a unit. They were by themselves, or maybe a half dozen, and they went through some separation center, and that's all. They went back to their homes. It was like there was no end to it. I'm sure it must have been a letdown for them, they were just glad to get out. But there was no recognition, which we didn't have.[5]

Staff Sergeant James Walsh, a machine gunner with the Army's 25th Infantry Division and winner of the Bronze Star and the Purple Heart, expressed similar sentiments on his return to the United States:

> I rotated back to the good old USA in May 1952, an alive, very bright, single-rocker U.S. Army staff sergeant.
>
> It took two weeks for the troop ship to cross the Pacific Ocean. When it docked at San Francisco's Presidio, it nearly keeled over, every GI who could crowding the rails dockside. We looked for the welcoming committee, a band, the Red Cross with coffee and donuts.
>
> There was no crowd, no band, no Red Cross, no coffee or donuts, nothing to welcome America's fighting

Catherine Neville, in a photograph taken in 2001. This veteran of World War II, the Korean War, and the Vietnam War was interviewed as part of the Veterans Oral History Project of the Library of Congress, an ongoing project supported by the United States Congress to gather the stories of American veterans of war and civilians who supported war efforts.

men home from Korea in late May 1952. There was a collective grunt for ingratitude.

The ship's unloading ramp hit the landing, and GI's, thrilled to be back on American soil while irritated they'd been forgotten, filed cheerfully toward the reception building. From out of nowhere, three civilians, a beautiful young woman dressed prettier than a fashion model and an older pretty woman, as sharply dressed holding the hand of an older handsome man in a black serge suit and red tie, rushed onto the landing. A GI broke ranks and ran from the ramp into the arms of his sweetheart, his parents. They hugged and kissed, kissed and hugged, hugged and kissed.

There wasn't a dry GI eye aboard the ship or on the landing.[6]

"The Worst and the Best"

Regardless of the homecoming they received, most of the men and women who were involved in the Korean War were affected by it for the rest of their lives. Paul Steppe recalled the bitterness that lingered for some of his Marine Corps buddies, but he believed that the war and his part in it had not been in vain.

I had a little leather binder that had all the addresses of my buddies. When I got hurt, that was lost. I didn't have any addresses, and when I wanted to get in touch with them, I'd forgotten their last names. I contacted one from Maryland, and he didn't even want to talk to me. He wanted to forget it. And there are probably a lot of people out there like that that don't want to talk about what we're talking about today. . . .

The smell of the bodies always stays with you. One time I was running over a hill and a machine gun was following me, and I thought, I'm sure he's gonna get me. So I stopped. And he stopped. And then I started running different paces, slow and fast; he couldn't keep up with me. I was grateful that he was a bad shot. I jumped into this big hole and the hole was full of dead body pieces. I had to stay there all night by myself. I had dropped my flamethrower before I went over this ridge.

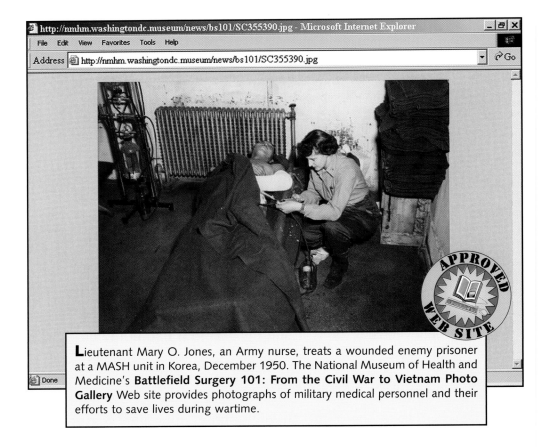

http://nmhm.washingtondc.museum/news/bs101/SC355390.jpg - Microsoft Internet Explorer

File   Edit   View   Favorites   Tools   Help

Address http://nmhm.washingtondc.museum/news/bs101/SC355390.jpg

Lieutenant Mary O. Jones, an Army nurse, treats a wounded enemy prisoner at a MASH unit in Korea, December 1950. The National Museum of Health and Medicine's **Battlefield Surgery 101: From the Civil War to Vietnam Photo Gallery** Web site provides photographs of military medical personnel and their efforts to save lives during wartime.

War brings out the worst and the best in us. Sometimes you're arrogant and you don't wish to be arrogant. Sometimes you're nasty and you don't wish to be nasty. A lot of veterans turned to alcohol because they couldn't make those decisions. . . .

That Korean time was the most fabulous time of America. America was trying to get back on its feet from a four-year war, and all of a sudden we're hit with this invasion of South Korea, and troops came to the call. So that was a fine, fine moment for America right then.[7]

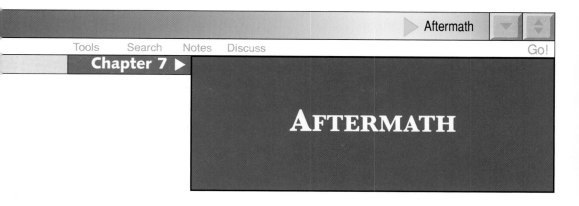

AFTERMATH

The Korean War devastated the Korean peninsula. Nearly 4 million Korean civilians were killed or wounded and another 5 million were made refugees. The South Korean forces suffered 220,000 casualties, plus another 80,000 captured by Communist forces, and many of them died in captivity.[1] The United States suffered 33,600 killed and more than 100,000 wounded.[2] The North Korean military

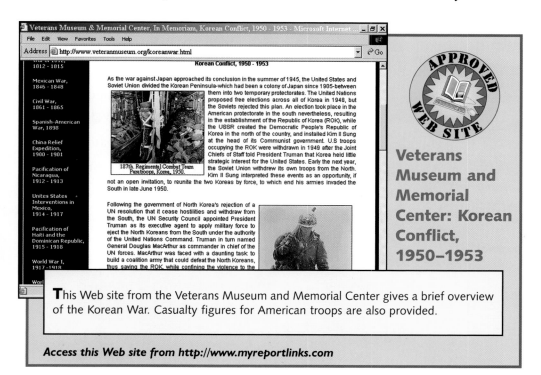

This Web site from the Veterans Museum and Memorial Center gives a brief overview of the Korean War. Casualty figures for American troops are also provided.

Access this Web site from http://www.myreportlinks.com

lost 600,000 men. While no exact numbers exist for Chinese troops, it is assumed that there were more than a million casualties.[3]

The border between the two Korean states was drawn at the line of contact at the end of the war and remains at that line. There is a demilitarized zone between the countries, and its borders are heavily patrolled.[4]

Kim Il Sung remained in control of North Korea and tightened his grip on the country. Through propaganda broadcasts that told North Koreans that North Korea had won the Korean War, he remained in power and passed his dictatorship on to his son, Kim Jong Il, the ruler of North Korea.

Syngman Rhee succeeded in obtaining significant American support for South Korea, including a mutual defense pact and the stationing of the U.S. Eighth Army in South Korea for nearly half a century. The United States would not sanction Rhee's plans to reunify the peninsula by force, however. The constant threat of the renewal of hostilities pushed Rhee to abuse his power and spend enormous amounts on the military, which slowed his country's economic recovery. Rhee was overthrown in 1960.[5]

▶ Arguments Against Defeat

Many historians argue that since Korea remained divided following the war, with the Communists still in charge of the North, the Korean War was essentially a UNC defeat, but the UNC did accomplish some of its objectives. All of the major UNC demands were met in the cease-fire negotiations. The line of contact rather than the 38th parallel became the border between North Korea and South Korea. The UNC suffered far fewer losses in men and equipment than the Communist forces did.

Most importantly, the Korean War halted overt Communist aggression. The governments of the Soviet Union and China pursued a less aggressive foreign policy. Conflicts with the United States were handled through proxy countries, smaller countries backed by the Communists or the United States. There were no more direct confrontations, and both sides were careful not to allow any of these smaller conflicts escalate into a larger war.

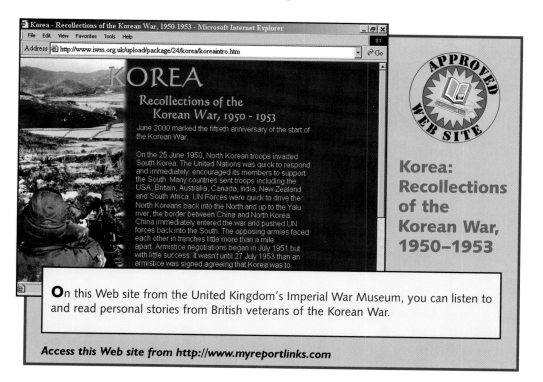

Korea: Recollections of the Korean War, 1950–1953

On this Web site from the United Kingdom's Imperial War Museum, you can listen to and read personal stories from British veterans of the Korean War.

Access this Web site from http://www.myreportlinks.com

Military Gains and Losses

The American armed forces came out of the Korean War convinced that superior firepower, equipment, and technology could compensate for any weakness or shortcoming in training. Unfortunately, the United States repeated many of the same mistakes it made in Korea just a decade later in the war in Vietnam.[6] The isolated terrain of Korea allowed the UNC time to correct mistakes made in the field and make up for poor performance by keeping the lines of defense short. In Vietnam, there were no short lines of defense, and the same minor mistakes in Korea became major fatal mistakes in Vietnam.

The Communist forces came out of the Korean War with more profitable lessons. Mao Zedong learned that it would take more than political indoctrination and guerrilla warfare to defeat western armies, even if Communist forces were willing to accept heavy casualties. The CPV learned that it could not face a western army on its own terms—Communist armies should fight only when western technological advantages were minimized.[7] The Communist forces also learned to exploit the greatest weakness of any democracy: the impatience of its citizens.[8] Most importantly, China came out of the Korean War as an acknowledged world power.

Other Beneficiaries

The war helped to revitalize the North Atlantic Treaty Organization (NATO), a military alliance of

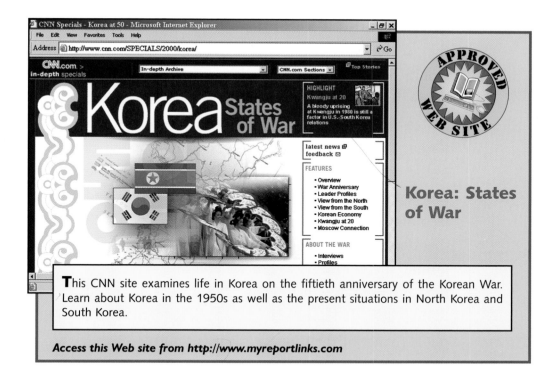

CNN Specials - Korea at 50 - Microsoft Internet Explorer

File   Edit   View   Favorites   Tools   Help

Address http://www.cnn.com/SPECIALS/2000/korea/   Go

CNN.com >
in-depth specials

In-depth Archive   CNN.com Sections   Top Stories

Korea States of War

HIGHLIGHT
Kwangju at 20
A bloody uprising
at Kwangju in 1980 is still a
factor in U.S.-South Korea
relations

latest news
feedback

FEATURES
• Overview
• War Anniversary
• Leader Profiles
• View from the North
• View from the South
• Korean Economy
• Kwangju at 20
• Moscow Connection

ABOUT THE WAR
• Interviews
• Profiles

Korea: States of War

APPROVED
WEB SITE

This CNN site examines life in Korea on the fiftieth anniversary of the Korean War. Learn about Korea in the 1950s as well as the present situations in North Korea and South Korea.

Access this Web site from http://www.myreportlinks.com

countries from Europe and North America formed by a treaty in 1949.[9] The militaries of the United States and its allies were kept strong in the face of the threat imposed by Communism. The money that poured into Japan during the war helped the Japanese recover and rebuild following the devastation of World War II and greatly assisted Japan's return as a world economic power.[10]

▷ The Soviet Union's Role

The Soviets used Korea as an experiment to test the resolve of the United States in defending its allies. While the Soviet Union may not have encouraged North Korea's invasion of South Korea, its consent was needed for it to happen. There is some doubt that the Soviets really believed the United States would respond to the invasion, but there is little doubt that the Soviets did not expect the United States to invest as much as it did to protect South Korea. The Soviets never again boycotted meetings of the UN Security Council (their boycott had made the vote sending UN troops to Korea possible) and also never underestimated the lengths to which the United States would go to defend its interests around the world.[11] The Korean War also represents the only time in which Soviet and American armed forced faced off directly. That happened with Soviet pilots flying for the Chinese Air Force until 1953.

The relationships between Communist regimes in the Soviet Union and China were permanently damaged because of the division created by the Korean War. Promised aid from the Soviets arrived late, and the Chinese resented having to pay for it.[12] A gap of trust opened that did not heal until the breakup of the Soviet Union in 1991.

The Koreas

South Korea has emerged as one of the most modern countries in Asia, an economic and industrial power in its own right.[13] The threat from North Korea has never subsided; North Korea continues to try to undermine South Korea through secret operations and occasional acts of terrorism. There is still a strong United States military presence in

Seoul, South Korea, has grown into a bustling, modern capital city whose inhabitants enjoy a much higher standard of living than their North Korean counterparts in Pyongyang.

South Korea, and the South Korean military itself is unusually large for a democracy. Just as Japan benefited from the Korean War, South Korea benefited from the Vietnam War a generation later.[14]

More than fifty years after the armistice, North Korea continues to pay a heavy price. Huge sections of the countryside that were devastated by the war have not been rebuilt. North Korea remains one of

▲ The Korean War, like all wars, brought suffering to the most innocent of victims, children.

the most repressive and backward societies in the world. Years of mismanagement and financing a military of more than one million men has forced it to rely on international aid to feed its population. While China has westernized its economy and opened its doors to new markets, North Korea remains the "Hermit Kingdom." Its people live in stark poverty and in isolation from the rest of the world, and its government is ruled by an unstable dictator.

A Small Sign of Hope

For Koreans whose families were divided by the war, most had no contact for nearly fifty years because South Koreans could not enter the North, and North Koreans could not leave their own country. In 2000, the leaders of the North and South agreed to make some visits across the DMZ possible. Since then, thousands of Koreans who had not seen relatives for decades have been reunited. It is still the hope of many Koreans to see their country reunified.

Report Links

The Internet sites described below can be accessed at
http://www.myreportlinks.com

▶ **Dwight D. Eisenhower Presidential Library: Primary Sources—The Korean War**
Editor's Choice View primary source documents and photographs from the Korean War.

▶ **Korea+50: No Longer Forgotten**
Editor's Choice Presidential libraries offer an examination of the Korean War.

▶ *American Experience: MacArthur*
Editor's Choice Explore the military career of General Douglas MacArthur.

▶ **Wisconsin War Letters: The Korean War**
Editor's Choice Read letters written by soldiers from Wisconsin who fought in Korea.

▶ *American Experience: War Letters*
Editor's Choice Read letters written by American veterans of the Korean War.

▶ **Veterans History Project**
Editor's Choice This Library of Congress site presents first-person accounts of American veterans.

▶ **Battlefield Surgery 101: From the Civil War to Vietnam Photo Gallery**
View images of wartime medical care on this site.

▶ **British Battles: Korea, 1951**
Learn about Britain's involvement in the Korean War from the National Archives of the United Kingdom.

▶ **Cold War International History Project—Korean War**
This site features Korean War telegrams and memos documenting the Soviet Union's involvement.

▶ **Cold War: Korea: 1949–1953**
Explore the Korean War on this Web site from CNN.

▶ **Digitized Primary American History Sources**
View a collection of primary sources of American history.

▶ **Korean War**
Military maps of Korean War campaigns are found on this West Point Web site.

▶ **Korea: Recollections of the Korean War, 1950–1953**
Listen to Korean War stories from some of the British soldiers who fought in it.

▶ **Korea: States of War**
Find out about life in Korea fifty years after war broke out.

▶ **Korea: The Forgotten War**
This newspaper site offers an interactive exhibit of America's "Forgotten War."

Report Links

The Internet sites described below can be accessed at http://www.myreportlinks.com

▶**Named Campaigns—Korean War**
The U.S. Army's Center of Military History Web site gives a brief overview of the war's battles.

▶**National Archives: The United States Enters the Korean Conflict**
The background of events leading to the Korean War and an archival document are presented.

▶**National Park Service: Korean War Veterans Memorial**
Visit the Web site of the Korean War Veterans Memorial.

▶**1950s: The Korean War in Popular Culture**
Browse through this collection of cartoons and comic books with Korean War themes.

▶**Online Bookshelves: Korean War**
Read these military history texts of the Korean War.

▶**Our Documents: Armistice Agreement**
Read the armistice agreement that ended the fighting in the Korean War.

▶**The Price of Freedom: Americans at War**
View Korean War artifacts from the National Museum of American History.

▶**Recollections of War: "Maurie" Pears**
Read this personal account of the Korean War from an Australian soldier.

▶**United States of America: Korean War Commemoration**
Visit this Web site commemorating the fiftieth anniversary of the Korean War.

▶**USAF: Korean War 50th Anniversary**
Learn about the United States Air Force's participation in the Korean War.

▶**U.S. Centennial of Flight Commission: The Korean War**
Read about the use of airpower during the Korean War.

▶**U.S. Marine Corps: Korean War Commemoration**
Learn about the role of the U.S. Marines in the Korean War.

▶**U.S. Navy: The Korean War**
View Korean War images from the Web site of the Naval Historical Center.

▶**Veterans Museum and Memorial Center: Korean Conflict, 1950–1953**
Read a brief overview of the war on this Web site dedicated to veterans.

▶***Wide Angle: A State of Mind:* Time Line of the Korean War**
A PBS site examines the Korean War from North Korea's perspective.

ammo—A shortened term for ammunition, such as bullets and cartridges; also grenades.

amphibious assault—An attack conducted over water and onto land.

aperture—An opening or hole.

armistice—A truce or temporary stoppage of hostilities.

attrition—The act of weakening or exhausting.

bivouac—Temporary shelter or camp.

British Commonwealth Division—The combined forces of Great Britain and its former colonies of Canada, Australia, and New Zealand. The British Commonwealth Division played a major role in the war (especially at the defense of Imjin River) and performed superbly as perhaps the best UNC forces of the Korean War.

Browning Automatic Rifle—Also known as a BAR or B.A.R., it was used by the U.S. Army infantry as a light machine gun.

casualties—Military personnel lost in a war through death, combat wounds, injury, illness, and imprisonment. Included are those missing in action.

cease-fire—An order to stop firing, or end active fighting in a war zone.

corpsmen—Enlisted people who provide medical assistance in combat for the Marines and Navy; the Army calls such personnel medics.

CPV—Chinese People's Volunteers, the Chinese Army that fought in Korea.

demilitarized zone—Also known as the DMZ. A demilitarized zone is an area where military personnel, installations, and operations are permitted to create a buffer between two states. Korea's DMZ, which runs for 155 miles, was originally situated along the 38th parallel but was moved to the line of contact at the end of the Korean War.

F–86 Sabre—The F–86 Sabre was the premiere UNC jet fighter of the Korean War, the only fighter that was a match for the Soviet-built MiG–15. By the end of the war, Sabres had shot down 792 MiGs while losing only 76 Sabres in combat.

gook—An insulting term for an enemy soldier, either Chinese or North Korean.

guerrillas—Fighters who use unconventional tactics such as hiding, harassing, and sabotage.

infantry—Soldiers trained and equipped to fight on foot; also a regiment or division of such soldiers.

limited war—A conflict in which both sides have restrictions on the criteria for victory short of total defeat of the enemy. The means of fighting the war may also exclude certain weapons, tactics, and territories in order to achieve victory.

magazine—A bullet or cartridge holder.

MASH—A Mobile Army Surgical Hospital.

MiG–15—The MiG–15 (named for Soviet aircraft builders Mikoyan and Gurevich) was a stable, dependable jet fighter flown by Communist forces during the Korean War. Its appearance in the skies proved a shock to UNC forces because the MiG–15 was a much better fighter than the standard UNC F–80 Shooting Star. The MiG–15 was fast, cheap to build, and easy to fly.

monsoon—A season in certain parts of the world in which wind conditions bring about heavy rains.

MLR—Main Line of Resistance, the front line of combat between the UNC and Communist forces.

munitions—Weapons.

NCO—Noncommissioned Officer; a subordinate officer, such as a sergeant, in the military chosen from among enlisted men.

offensive—An attack.

platoon—A military unit smaller than a company, usually made up of two or more squads.

police action—Formally, Korea was not a war, since no official declarations of war were made by either side. President Truman called the combat in Korea a "police action," referring to an enforcement of international law.

propaganda—Ideas, allegations, and rumors spread to further one's cause and damage an opposing cause.

ROK—The Republic of Korea, or South Korea; also refers to the soldiers in its army.

stalemate—A point at which neither side in a contest has the upper hand and no progress is being made.

Chapter 1. A Stand on Pork Chop Hill

1. Bill McWilliams, *On Hallowed Ground: The Last Battle for Pork Chop Hill* (New York: Berkeley Caliber Books, 2004), p. 214. Originally published 2004, Naval Institute Press. Used with permission.

2. Ibid., p. 218.

3. Ibid., pp. 327–328.

4. Ibid., pp. 330–331.

5. James I. Marino, "Meat Grinder on Pork Chop Hill," *Military History* magazine, April 2003.

6. McWilliams., pp. 438–439.

Chapter 2. A Brief History of the Korean War

1. Allan Millet, *The War for Korea 1945–1950* (Lawrence: University of Kansas Press, 2005), pp. 50–52.

2. Max Hastings, *The Korean War* (New York: Simon & Schuster, 1987), p. 27.

3. Millet, p. 68.

4. Ibid., p. 126.

5. Hastings, pp. 41–42.

6. Carter Malkasian, *The Korean War 1950–1953* (Oxford, U.K.: Osprey Publishing Limited, 2001), p. 13.

7. Millet, p. 303.

8. Michael Hickey, *The Korean War: The West Confronts Communism* (Woodstock, N.Y.: Overlook Press, 2000), p. 26.

9. Malkasian, p. 14.

10. Millet, pp. 241–244.

11. Malkasian, pp. 15–16.

12. Millet, p. 244.

13. Malkasian, p. 16.

14. Steven Hugh Lee, *The Korean War* (Harlow, U.K.: Pearson Education Ltd., 2001), p. 91.

15. Hastings, pp. 84–89.

16. Ibid., pp. 99–103.

17. Lee, p. 50.

18. Ibid., pp. 51–52.
19. Malkasian, p. 54.
20. Hastings, p. 122.
21. Ibid., p. 133.
22. Malkasian, p. 32.
23. Lee, p. 53.
24. Malkasian, pp. 33–34.
25. Hastings, p. 164.
26. Malkasian, p. 36.
27. Ibid.
28. Hastings, pp. 178–182.
29. Hickey, p. 125.
30. Malkasian, p. 39.
31. Hickey, p. 220.
32. Hickey, pp. 196–197.
33. Malkasian, p. 41.
34. Hickey, pp. 230–235.
35. Lee, p. 84.
36. Hastings, pp. 231–233.
37. Ibid., p. 258.
38. Ibid., pp. 266–267.
39. Malkasian, p. 60.
40. Lee, pp. 87–88.
41. Ibid., pp. 86–87.
42. Hastings, pp. 293–294.
43. Ibid., p. 301.
44. Ibid., pp. 308–309.
45. Ibid., pp. 310–311.
46. Lee, pp. 91–92.
47. Hickey, p. 335.
48. Ibid.
49. Hastings, pp. 323–324.
50. Ibid., p. 325.

51. The National Park Service, The Korean War Veterans Memorial, "Preamble," *Agreement Between the Commander-In-Chief, United Nations Command, on the One Hand, and the Supreme Commander of the Korean People's Army and the Commander of the Chinese People's Volunteers, on the Other Hand, Concerning a Military Armistice in Korea, July 27, 1953,* <http://www.nps.gov /kwvm/war/1953.htm> (May 6, 2006).

Chapter 3. Life on the Front

1. James Brady, *The Coldest War: A Memoir of Korea* (New York: St. Martin's Griffin, 2000), p. 111.

2. Ibid., p. 112.

3. Steven Hugh Lee, *The Korean War* (Harlow, U.K.: Pearson Education Ltd., 2001), p. 144.

4. Tom Wiener, ed., *Voices of War: Stories of Service From the Home Front and the Front Lines* (Washington, D.C.: The National Geographic Society, 2004), p. 72.

5. Brady, pp. 114–115.

6. Ibid.

7. Joseph R. Owen, *Colder Than Hell: A Marine Rifle Company at Chosin Reservoir* (New York: Random House, 1997), pp. 212–213.

8. Wiener, p. 151.

9. University of Wisconsin-Milwaukee, *Wisconsin War Letters,* Frank Griepp, December 2, 1950, <http://www.uwm .edu/Library/arch/Warletters/korea/griepp.htm> (May 6, 2006).

Chapter 4. Under Fire and Imprisoned

1. Joseph R. Owen, *Colder Than Hell: A Marine Rifle Company at Chosin Reservoir* (New York: Random House, 1997), pp. 177–179.

2. Ibid.

3. Tom Wiener, ed., *Voices of War: Stories of Service From the Home Front and the Front Lines* (Washington, D.C.: The National Geographic Society, 2004), p. 152.

4. Ibid.

5. Ibid., p. 153.

6. Owen, p. 213.

7. Andrew Carroll, *Behind the Lines: Powerful and Revealing American and Foreign War Letters—And One Man's Search to Find Them* (New York: Scribner's, 2005), p. 178.

8. United States Department of Defense, Korean War Commemoration, "The Lucky One," Harley Coon as told to Navy Chief Journalist Milinda D. Jensen, 50th Anniversary Korean War Commemoration Committee, 2003, <http://korea50.army.mil /media/interviews/coon.shtml> (May 6, 2006).

9. Ibid.

10. Ibid.

11. Ibid.

12. Ibid.

13. American RadioWorks, *Korea: The Unfinished War,* Stephen Smith and Sasha Aslanian, producers, "The Armed Forces Integrate," July 2003, <http://americanradioworks .publicradio.org/features/korea/b5.htm> (May 2, 2006). Copyright 2003, American Public Media. All rights reserved. Reproduced with permission of American Public Media.

14. Ibid.

15. Ibid.,<http://americanradioworks.publicradio.org /features/korea/b4.html> (May 6, 2006).

Chapter 5. The Politics of War and the American Public

1. Harry Truman, *Years of Trial and Hope, Memoirs by Harry S Truman* (New York: Doubleday, 1965), pp. 378–379.

2. Harry Truman, Truman Presidential Museum and Library, "Desegregation of the Armed Forces," *Executive Order 9981,* July 26, 1948, <http://www.trumanlibrary.org/whistlestop/study _collections/desegregation/large/index.php?action=chronology > (May 6, 2006).

3. Steven Hugh Lee, *The Korean War* (Harlow, U.K.: Pearson Education Ltd., 2001), p. 132.

4. Ibid., p. 141.

5. John Gittings, *The Role of the Chinese Army* (London: Oxford University Press, 1967), pp. 133–134.

6. US National Archives, OSS and State Department Numbered Intelligence Reports, 1941–1961, Report No. 6062.

Chapter 6. Coming Home

1. Andrew Carroll, *Behind the Lines: Powerful and Revealing American and Foreign War Letters—And One Man's Search to Find Them* (New York: Scribner's, 2005), pp. 417–419.

2. Ibid.

3. Ibid.

4. Ibid.

5. Tom Wiener, ed., *Voices of War: Stories of Service From the Home Front and the Front Lines* (Washington, D.C.: The National Geographic Society, 2004), p. 279.

6. Ibid., pp. 282–283.

7. Ibid., pp. 309–310.

Chapter 7. Aftermath

1. Carter Malkasian, *The Korean War 1950–1953* (Oxford, U.K.: Osprey Publishing Limited, 2001), p. 88.

2. Max Hastings, *The Korean War* (New York: Simon & Schuster, 1987), p. 329.

3. Ibid.

4. Michael Hickey, *The Korean War: The West Confronts Communism* (Woodstock, N.Y.: Overlook Press, 2000), p. 360.

5. Hastings, p. 343.

6. Ibid., pp. 333–334.

7. Ibid., pp. 335–336.

8. Ibid.

9. Malkasian, p. 91.

10. Steven Hugh Lee, *The Korean War* (Harlow, U.K.: Pearson Education Ltd., 2001), pp. 102–104.

11. Hastings, p. 340.

12. Malkasian, pp. 91–92.

13. Hastings, pp. 342–343.

14. Ibid., p. 343.

Ashabranner, Brent. *Remembering Korea: The Korean War Veterans Memorial.* Brookfield, Conn.: Twenty-First Century Books, 2001.

Dubois, Jill. *Korea.* New York: Benchmark Books/Marshall Cavendish, 2005.

Gaines, Ann Graham. *Douglas MacArthur: Brilliant General, Controversial Leader.* Berkeley Heights, N.J.: Enslow Publishers, Inc., 2001.

Granfield, Linda. *I Remember Korea: Veterans Tell Their Stories of the Korean War 1950–53.* Markham, Ont.: Fitzhenry & Whiteside, 2004.

Isserman, Maurice. *Korean War: Updated Edition.* New York: Facts on File, 2003.

Lindop, Edmund. *America in the 1950s.* Brookfield, Conn.: Twenty-First Century Books, 2002.

Nishi, Dennis, ed. *The Korean War.* San Diego: Greenhaven Press, 2003.

Sherman, Josepha. *The Cold War.* Minneapolis: Lerner Publications, 2004.

Sullivan, George. *Journalists at Risk: Reporting America's Wars.* Minneapolis: Twenty-First Century Books, 2006.

White, Matt. *Cameras on the Battlefield: Photos of War.* Mankato, Minn.: Capstone Curriculum Pub., 2002.

A

Able Company,
17th Infantry, 15
accounts
battles (*See individual battle by name*)
homecoming, 101–105
prisoners of war, 78–82
refugees, Korean, 67–69
soldier (*See* soldiers' accounts, UNC)
of Syngman Rhee, 88–89
African Americans, 83–85
air strikes, UNC, 7, 44–45
armistice
protest of, 52, 54
signing of, 7, 54–55
atomic weapons, 25, 26, 29, 51, 52
Attlee, Clement, 37

B

Brady, James, 56–58, 61, 62
brainwashing, 48, 96
Brush, Ted, 77–78

C

Cannon, John, 85
casualties
Chinese, 39, 108
North Korean, 107–108
totals, 23
UNC troops, 10, 18, 107
cease-fire negotiations
leverage, attempts at, 11, 12
opening of, 6, 7, 43–44, 47, 51–52
protests of, 7, 52, 54
suspension of, 7, 43
Cheju-do, 23
Chiang Kai-shek, 24
China
aftermath of war, 109, 110, 112, 115
communism in, 24–25
home situation of, 51
negotiation tactics of, 11, 12, 43, 44
as North Korean ally, 32–33
operative in POW uprising, 49
prisoners of war, 47
war declaration by, 6

war tactics of, 15, 33–34, 39–40, 84
Chinese People's Volunteers (CPV)
aftermath of war, 110
in the Fifth Offensive, 41, 43
initial involvement of, 32
negotiation tactics of, 51–52
and prisoners of war, 48
retreat of, 44
supply issues of, 91–92
war tactics of, 34–37, 39
Chosin Reservoir, Battle of
about, 6, 36–37
accounts of, 62–66
Clark, Mark
as UNC head, 7, 46
war tactics of, 50–51
Combat Squad, 95
comic books, 96
Coon, Harley, 79–82

D

dams, bombing of, 7, 52
defeat, arguments against, 108–109
demilitarized zone (DMZ), 16, 108
Democratic People's Republic of Korea (North Korea)
aftermath of war, 108, 112–115
establishment of, 6
home situation of, 51
negotiation tactics of, 11, 12
retreat of, 32
victories, initial, 29–30
Dodd, Francis, 7, 50

E

Eisenhower, Dwight D., 7, 50–52
Exe, Dwight, 60
Executive Order 9981, 83, 87–88

F

families, reunification of, 115
F-86 Sabre, 44
Fifth Phase Offensive, 6, 40–43

First Phase Offensive, 6, 34–35
Fixed Bayonets, 95
Fourth Phase Offensive, 6, 39

G

George Company, 17th Infantry, 13, 14
Gloucester Regiment, 40–41
Great Britain, role of, 30, 37
Griepp, Frank, 67–69

H

Hill 255. *See* Pork Chop Hill, Battle of.
homecoming, 98, 101–105
honor, retaining, 12
hydroelectric plants, bombing of, 7, 46–47

I

Inchon, landings at, 6, 30–31, 71
intelligence efforts, UNC, 92–93

J

Japan, 6, 21, 111
Jones, Mary, 106

K

Kansas Line, 40, 44
Kim Il Sung
aftermath of war, 108
election of, 23
and Soviet military aid, 24–25
war tactics of, 47
King, Samuel, 84
Koje-do uprising, 7, 49–50
Korea
division of, 6, 21
elections in, 22–23
Korean War
aftermath, 107–108
battle sites of, 8, 11, 39
beginning of, 23, 26, 28
motivations for, 20–22, 25–26
phases of, 28–29
time line, 6–7
Kumsong Bulge, Battle of the, 7, 52

L

Lee, Chew Een, 70–73
letters regarding fallen soldiers, 16–19

leverage, attempts at, 11, 12
limited war, 29, 37–38, 95
Lorenz, Martin, 9, 15, 19

M

MacArthur, Douglas
  dismissal of, 6, 40, 41
  as UNC head, 6, 28
  war tactics of, 30–31,
    33–38
mail call, 59–62
Main Line of Resistance
  (MLR), 11, 67
Manchuria, 32
The Manchurian Candidate,
  95–96
Mao Zedong, 24, 32, 47, 110
M*A*S*H*, 96–97
media views on war, 95–97
medics, methods of, 77
MiG-15, 44, 45
military gains/losses, 110
Morrow, Curtis, 84
Moscow Conference, 21

N

negotiation tactics
  of China, 11, 12, 43, 44
  of the CPV, 51–52
  of North Korea, 11, 12
  Soviet Union, 6, 7, 43
Neville, Catherine, 102,
  103, 104
North Atlantic Treaty
  Organization (NATO),
  110–111
North Korea. *See* Democratic
  People's Republic
  of Korea.

O

Old Baldy (hill), battle for, 7
Operation Commando, 7
Operation Fishnet, 92
Operation Thunderbolt,
  6, 38–40
Owen, Joseph, 62–63, 66,
  70–73, 76–77

P

Pak Hon Yong, 88–89
Palermo, Angel, 15–16
Panmunjom, peace
  negotiations in, 7, 12,
  44, 47
Pears, Maurie, 58–59

Phillips, John, 13–14
political indoctrination,
  48, 96
politics of war
  American public, 95
  Korean views, 88–89
  UNC views, 86–88
Pork Chop Hill, 95
Pork Chop Hill, Battle of
  about, 7, 9–11
  accounts of, 11–19
prisoners of war
  accounts, daily life,
    78–82
  Chinese/North Korean,
    life of, 49
  Koje-do uprising,
    7, 49–50
  in negotiations, 47, 54
  UNC, life of, 47–48,
    78–82
public views, American, 95
Puntasecca, Al, 98–101
Pusan Perimeter, battles of,
  6, 30, 32
Pyongyang, bombing of,
  7, 47

R

racial integration in
  American armed
  services, 83, 87–88
refugees, Korean, 67–69
Republic of Korea (South
  Korea)
  aftermath of war,
    108, 112–115
  establishment of, 6
  invasion of, 6, 26
  protests by, 7
Rhee, Syngman. *See*
  Syngman Rhee.
Ridgway, Matthew
  military tactics of, 44
  as UNC head, 6, 40

S

saving face, 12
Second Phase Offensive,
  6, 35–36
2nd U.S. Infantry Division,
  35–36
Seoul, battle for, 32, 40–43
17th Infantry Unit, 7, 13

Shea, Richard, 11–13,
  16–17, 19
soldiers' accounts, UNC
  attitudes, changes in, 100
  being wounded,
    75–78, 101
  bigotry, 85
  Chinese propaganda, 84
  combat, 70–74
  daily life, 56–58
  homecoming, 98–99,
    103–104
  mail call, 59–62
  memories of war,
    105–106
  North Korean war
    effort, 93
  Pork Chop Hill, 11–19
  as POWs, 80–82
  trench warfare, 58–59
  war in general,
    74–76, 101
  weather conditions,
    62–67, 76–77
songs of war, 97
South Korea. *See* Republic
  of Korea.
Soviet Union
  aftermath of war,
    109, 111–112
  military support by,
    25–26, 32–33
  negotiation tactics by,
    6, 7, 43
  and North Korea, 6,
    21, 25–26
  UN membership,
    23, 112
  and UNTOK, 22
Stalin, Joseph
  on armistice, 47
  death of, 7, 51
  military support by,
    25–26, 32–33
  motivations of, 51
Steppe, Paul, 59, 61, 67,
  73–75, 105–106
Struble, Arthur Dewey,
  31–32
supply lines, cutting, 91–92
Syngman Rhee
  accounts of, 88–89
  aftermath of war, 108
  election of, 23

POW release by, 54
on war escalation,
89–91

T

tactics of negotiation. *See*
negotiation tactics.
tactics of war, 28–29
of China, 15, 33–34,
39–40, 84
Clark, Mark, 50–51
of CPV, 34–37, 39
of Kim Il Sung, 47
MacArthur, Douglas,
30–31, 33–38
Ridgway, Matthew, 44
Truman, Harry S,
33–34, 37
United Nations
Command, 30,
33–34, 46–47,
52, 91–92
United States, 38
technology in war, 110
Third Phase Offensive, 6, 39
38th parallel, 6, 9, 21, 34
31st Infantry Regiment, 7
trench warfare, 14, 16,
58–59
Truman, Harry S
image of, 27

integration orders of,
83, 87–88
negotiations, account
of, 42
political tactics of,
86–87
UN resolutions and, 28
Wake Island meeting, 6
war tactics of, 33–34, 37
29th Commonwealth
Brigade, 40
27th Commonwealth
Brigade, 40

U

Uijongbu, battle for, 40–43
United Nations, role of,
22–23, 28, 34
United Nations Command
(UNC)
aftermath of war,
108–109
air strikes, 7, 44–45
creation of, 6, 28
war tactics of, 30,
33–34, 46–47, 52,
91–92
United Nations Temporary
Commission on Korea
(UNTCOK), 22
United States

aftermath of war, 108,
110, 111
in Pusan, 30
in South Korea, 6,
21–22, 26, 28, 113
war tactics of, 38
U.S. Army 7th Infantry
Division, 7, 11
U.S. Marines, 31–32, 36–37

V

veterans, portrayal of,
96–97
Vietnam War, 95–97,
102–104, 106,
110, 113

W

Wake Island meeting, 6, 34
Walsh, James, 103–105
war of attrition, 28, 29, 45
war of maneuver, 28
war tactics. *See* tactics of war.
weather conditions, 62–67,
76–77

Y

Yalu River, 6, 34, 36, 37, 39.
See also Fifth Phase
Offensive; Second
Phase Offensive.

Photo Credits: © Corel Corporation, p. 113; AP/Wide World Photos, pp. 41, 50; Catherine Neville Collection (AFC/2001/001/113), Photographs (PH01), photographer unknown, Veterans History Project, American Folklife Center, Library of Congress. With the permission of Catherine Neville, pp. 102, 104; CNN Interactive, pp. 20, 111; Courtesy of Martin Lorenz, p. 19; Dwight D. Eisenhower Presidential Library, p. 57; Enslow Publishers, p. 8; Harry S Truman and Dwight D. Eisenhower Presidential Libraries, p. 79; Imperial War Museum, p. 109; Korea Remembered, p. 58; Library of Congress, p. 90; Library of Congress, Veterans History Project, p. 75; Martin Lorenz Collection (AFC/2001/001/2355), Veterans History Project, American Folklife Center, Library of Congress. With the permission of Martin Lorenz, pp. 9, 15; MyReportLinks.com Books, p. 4; National Archives and Records Administration, pp. 22, 42, 55; National Archives and Records Administration/Department of Defense, pp. 1, 3, 18, 27, 31, 33, 53, 60, 64–65, 66, 68, 71, 72, 81, 82–83, 94, 114; National Archives of the United Kingdom, p. 29; National Museum of Health and Medicine, p. 106; National Park Service, p. 100; PBS, pp. 38, 48, 99; Smithsonian Institution, p. 87; *St. Petersburg Times*, p. 36; The Authentic History Center, p. 96; The Cold War International History Project, p. 25; U.S. Centennial of Flight Commission, p. 46; United States Air Force Museum, p. 45; United States Army Center of Military History, pp. 11, 35, 39, 88; United States Department of Defense, p. 76; University of Northern Iowa, p. 24; University of Wisconsin, Madison, p. 69; U.S. Marine Corps, p. 63; U.S. Navy, Naval Historical Center, p. 92; Veterans Museum and Memorial Center, p. 107.